THE GOLDEN RULES
OF BLOGGING

(& WHEN TO BREAK THEM)

ROBIN
HOUGHTON

ilex

THE GOLDEN RULES OF BLOGGING (& WHEN TO BREAK THEM)

First published in the United Kingdom in 2015 by
ILEX
210 High Street
Lewes
East Sussex
BN7 2NS

Distributed worldwide (except North America)
by Thames & Hudson Ltd., 181A High Holborn,
London WC1V 7QX, United Kingdom

PUBLISHER: Alastair Campbell
EXECUTIVE PUBLISHER: Roly Allen
ASSOCIATE PUBLISHER: Adam Juniper
COMMISSIONING EDITOR: Zara Larcombe
EDITORIAL DIRECTOR: Nick Jones
SENIOR PROJECT EDITOR: Natalia Price-Cabrera
SENIOR SPECIALIST EDITOR: Frank Gallaugher
ASSISTANT EDITOR: Rachel Silverlight
ART DIRECTOR: Julie Weir
DESIGNER: Kate Haynes

British Library Cataloguing-in-Publication Data
A catalogue record for this book is available from
the British Library.

ISBN: 978-1-78157-239-9

Colour Origination by Ivy Press Reprographics

Printed and bound in China

10 9 8 7 6 5 4 3 2 1

CONTENTS:

INTRODUCTION
Do bloggers need rules?........6

#1 Blog for your target audience........8

#2 Always self-host........12

#3 Have a professional mind-set........16

#4 Check your stats regularly........20

#5 Post something every day........24

#6 Spelling & grammar mistakes will kill your blog........28

#7 Keep blog posts short........32

#8 Stick to one topic or niche........36

#9 Always end with a question........40

#10 Blog about your topic, not about yourself........44

THE GOLDEN RULES OF BLOGGING (& WHEN TO BREAK THEM)

#11 Don't be anonymous...............48

#12 Always include at least
one image................................52

#13 Avoid light text on a dark
background.............................56

#14 Killer headlines
are essential..........................60

#15 Publicize your blog
posts on social media.........64

#16 Comment regularly
on other blogs......................68

#17 Keep the look clean
& uncluttered.......................72

#18 Do not steal............................76

#19 Optimize every post
with keywords.......................80

#20 It's all about the
numbers..................................84

#21 Develop blogging buddies
....88

#22 Guest posting helps
with SEO.................................92

#23 Engage your audience
....96

#24 Anyone can make
money from blogging........100

#25 Build an email list.............104

#26 Make your content
shareable...............................108

#27 Ease up on the
hard sell.................................112

#28 Know all the rules
before you begin.................116

FINAL WORDS..............120
Resources...................................122
Index...126
Acknowledgments..................128

INTRODUCTION:
DO BLOGGERS NEED RULES?

DO YOU LIKE TO PLAY BY THE RULES? OR ARE RULEBOOKS FOR DUMMIES? A WISE PERSON ONCE SAID YOU CAN ONLY BREAK THE RULES IF YOU KNOW WHAT THEY ARE IN THE FIRST PLACE.

Of course, there are some rules you'd have to be crazy to break. Like "look both ways before crossing a railway line." But is that really true of blogging? It's amazing how many rules there seem to be, but the trouble is, for every rule there's an exception. How does a blogger make sense of it all?

The Golden Rules of Blogging & When to Break Them will help both experienced and beginner bloggers pick their way through the minefield of rules. Twenty-eight of the golden rules of blogging are laid bare—what they are, where they came from. Prepare to be surprised.

Some of these so-called rules have been set in stone by business gurus and web experts. Others come from bloggers who simply made them up as they went along. Yet more are throwbacks to a past age, before blogging and even before the web.

The problem is, not all rules are equal. Some you should take very seriously—but that doesn't mean you can't *ever* break them. Others are important for some bloggers, but not all. You'll see that the rules have been graded in terms of how risky it is to break them with an at-a-glance **Risk Factor** indicator for every rule.

I'll give you examples of when, why, and how to break the rules, as well as when you shouldn't. Some rules are more controversial than others, but the aim of this book is to empower bloggers with the knowledge they need to draw their own conclusions, rather than blindly following a set of often confusing rules.

Packed with blogging wisdom, *The Golden Rules of Blogging & When to Break Them* features real-life **Blogger Stories**, showing how it's not only possible to break the rules, but in many cases desirable. The book also features **Expert Comments** from those who have learned the hard way, all designed to guide the reader towards true twenty-first century blogging excellence.

Pro bloggers and hobby bloggers alike will all come away from this book with a different perspective on how to do it right, and the ability to decide for themselves which of the rules will be *their rules*.

#1 BLOG FOR YOUR TARGET AUDIENCE

**HAVE A CLEAR IDEA WHO YOU WANT TO READ YOUR BLOG,
AND TARGET YOUR BLOG POSTS TO THEIR INTERESTS.**

It stands to reason that if you want blog followers, you need to produce the stuff they want to read, watch, and share. Too many blogs are abandoned because the audience isn't responding as the blogger would like. So why labor on with a topic that clearly isn't setting the world on fire when you could be blogging about the things people want to read about. If you target your blog at a specific audience, comments and shares will improve, your audience will grow, and you'll start to make money from it. (*See also Rule #24.*)

Where it comes from:
This rule has its origin in business textbooks. Targeting is one of the basic tenets of marketing—don't try to appeal to everyone, it doesn't work. But if you target a section of the population, find out what they want to buy, and put yourself in their shoes, you're in with a chance. Many bloggers base their strategy on pre-internet business wisdom such as this.

WHEN TO BREAK THE RULE

Having a defined target audience isn't a bad idea in itself—it's the kind of advice I would give to any new blogger. It's certainly good to think about who you're blogging for. And much of that old-style business wisdom still has currency, especially if you're blogging for business reasons.

But maybe you just want to blog—you know, off-load what's on your mind or share a little wisdom on a subject you feel passionate about. Maybe you're not too worried about visitor numbers or comments, or lack thereof. You might be blogging for other reasons: as an experiment or exercise, or to hone your writing skills, or as a way of recording a project or a vacation, for your own pleasure or that of a small group of people.

If your reason for blogging is more to do with pleasing yourself than appealing to others, go ahead and forget about the target audience. The funny thing is, some blogs start out this way and go on to become very big and popular indeed.

"Write out of a desire to record and share experience and ideas."

—MICAH BALDWIN

RISK FACTOR: MEDIUM

BLOGGER STORY

"If you have a business blog, you should be targeting your ideal clients/ideal readers. If you sell food, then post recipes, review cooking equipment, and talk about the produce you sell. When readers come to your blog, they are expecting to find information about what services you offer and product information. Don't sell them short by posting about stuff that has nothing to do with your business—your reader will leave and never come back if you stray off topic too often. This also applies to advertising, if your blog carries ads. You won't make any money if you have buttons advertising luggage when you sell power tools. This gives your readers the impression you are just trying to make money from them instead of truly helping them.

"The main goal of your business blog should be to persuade people to come back, recommend you, share your content, and subscribe. A business blog that stays on target has the best chance of building a community, as people know exactly what to expect and they are never disappointed."

SARAH ARROW, WWW.SARKEMEDIA.COM

EXPERT COMMENT

"The moment when an experience or conversation makes you think to yourself, 'I should blog about that', is the exact moment you have become a blogger.

"Just because you write on a blog platform, you are not a blogger. A blogger is someone who wants to record their thoughts and experiences in an open format that others might read and enjoy (or even learn from). So, until a person sees the world in that context, she or he is not a blogger. She or he is just a writer.

"And fundamentally, that's the difference between the two. Bloggers want, invite, hope for two-way conversations to occur about what they write about. Writers just want people to read what they wrote. So is becoming a blogger that easy? Yes, it really is:

1) Write for yourself.
2) Write when you want to.
3) Write out of a desire to record and share experience and ideas.

"That's it."

MICAH BALDWIN, WWW.BLURB.COM

#2 ALWAYS SELF-HOST

YOU SHOULD ALWAYS OPT FOR A SELF-HOSTED BLOG RATHER THAN ONE THAT IS HOSTED AT (FOR EXAMPLE) WORDPRESS.COM OR BLOGGER.COM.

This is what all the professional bloggers do, and if you want to be found in searches, if you don't want to risk losing all your content, and if you want a professional-looking blog—then so should you.

Where it comes from:
This rule has become enshrined in blogger wisdom for several reasons. In the early days of blogging, hosted blogs offered few templates, and the look was somewhat homely. It's still the case that there are limitations to hosted blogs, varying according to the platform. A self-hosted blog, on the other hand, can be customized to your exact specifications. You have access to the open-source software that runs it, and to the server where it sits—it's all yours. You therefore have more control and ownership over its content.

"When you're self-hosted, you really own your website and have full control."

JANE FRIEDMAN

WHEN TO BREAK THE RULE

The hosted option is a lot more attractive today than it was in the early days of Blogger.

There are currently over 73 million blogs hosted at WordPress and well over 100 million at Tumblr, to name but two. So there are clearly quite a few people who are breaking this rule. Why? Here are the main reasons:

Security: The big blog hosts do a good job of keeping out the hackers and spammers. Whenever there's a software update, security upgrades are automatically installed. On a self-hosted blog, the blog software, your theme, and all the plug-ins need to be kept updated, and that's down to you. The consequences of not doing so can be serious—there are many happy IT people making a living from sorting out people's hacked blogs.

Design: Hosted blogs come with a good choice of free (or nearly free) templates or themes. They are well designed and work as they're supposed to, and the amount of customization you can do on them is surprisingly good.

Cost: You can have a basic hosted blog for free. The self-hosted option is never free, even though the blogging software itself may well be—you'll still need to pay for hosting and for development. With a hosted blog, you have the choice; if you want to pay for upgrades, you can.

RISK FACTOR: MEDIUM

#2 ALWAYS SELF-HOST

BLOGGER STORY

"Experts swear self-hosting is the cat's meow. They love it and advise that you too must do it in order to be a real blogger. I bought this rule hook, line, and sinker, with mixed results. I love my plug-ins. I love the feeling of ownership. However, I miss a few major perks from my days blogging on WordPress.com, such as regular updates, and themes that actually work. They do a great job of building community among their users. Turn-key. Worry-free. Cost-free. All that went away when I took the plunge to self-host.

"Now when I need to update my blog's look, I have to learn the technology to do it myself or hire someone to do it for me. And now I have to pay to have my blog up and running—forever and ever, amen. Not saying don't self-host. Just saying know what you're getting into and decide what's right for you."

AIMEE WHETSTINE, EVERYDAYEPISTLE.COM

EXPERT COMMENT

"There are several big reasons NOT to use a free service:

• Free services limit the functionality of your site.
• Free services limit how much you can customize the look and feel of the site.
• Sometimes you are working on proprietary systems that could be abandoned at any time. They might not be supported in the way you need them to be.
• Free services might not offer the kind of metrics and analytics you need in order to see what's working.
• It's more difficult to make money from a free service (it can be impossible to add an eCommerce/shopping cart functionality or to run ads).

"When you're self-hosted, you really own your website and have full control. And for serious, professional authors, who are building a long-term online presence, that's what I recommend."

JANE FRIEDMAN, JANEFRIEDMAN.COM

#3 HAVE A PROFESSIONAL MIND-SET

IF YOU'RE GOING TO BLOG, APPROACH IT AS IF YOU WERE A PROFESSIONAL WRITER BEING PAID FOR YOUR CONTENT-CREATION SKILLS. THERE ARE MILLIONS OF AMATEUR BLOGS OUT THERE, SO AIM HIGH IN TERMS OF QUALITY OF CONTENT IF YOU WANT READERS. SIMILARLY, THE MORE PROFESSIONAL-LOOKING YOUR BLOG IS, THE MORE LIKELY VISITORS WILL BE TO COME BACK.

Where it comes from:
This rule surfaces regularly on both business and creative blogs. "What a professional blog you've got!" is usually a compliment, particularly if you're blogging for business reasons, or if you're a writer looking to build your reputation and get paid work off the back of blogging. The accolade of "professional" is seen as a standard to aim for, and the "amateur" tag one to avoid. The first bloggers were amateur reporters, and subsequently the difference between journalism (professional writing) and blogging (amateur writing) has always been hotly debated.

When it comes to blog design, individual taste plays a big part. Anyone can start a blog, and although blogging platforms provide professionally designed templates, they can be modified, and the results aren't always pretty. Add to the mix a handful of user-created apps and widgets spilling out of the sidebars, and suddenly the whole thing starts to look distinctly amateur. The content itself may be valuable and unique, but too many of us are quick to judge a book by its cover. The gap between blog and regular website design has all but closed in recent years, and the homely blogs of yesteryear can appear dated.

WHEN TO BREAK THE RULE

Although the opposite of professional is amateur, it's worth remembering that the word amateur used to mean an "informed enthusiast" and didn't have the pejorative edge it now often has. Blogging is as much an outlet for the amateur as it is for the aspirant professional. And, in the eyes of the actual professionals in any given field, the pure blogger (as opposed to the "professional-who-blogs") will always be just that, never mind what his or her mind-set might be.

In short, if you want to make a business from blogging; if you want to appeal to advertisers or charge for content; if you want to win paid work on the basis of your blogged content, then a professional mind-set won't do you any harm. This means checking facts, eliminating errors, and presenting an appearance that doesn't seem homemade.

This doesn't mean that your blog needs to be corporate or impersonal, though. A blog should have passion and personality.

And if you're a hobby blogger, an enthusiast blogger, an I'm-doing-this-for-the-love blogger, by all means be as amateurish as you wish, and do with it just what you want.

RISK FACTOR: MEDIUM

BLOGGER STORY

"Blogging is whatever the blogger wants it to be. It can be a diary, a recipe folder, an art gallery, a clearing-house for other interesting sites—or it can be as true to journalistic standards as the writer presenting it makes it. I don't think there needs to be a dividing line. I also don't think the definition of a blogger is a writer who does it for free.

"A blog is meant to be more personal and informal than a piece written under strict journalistic, style-manual standards, but that doesn't mean it doesn't qualify as 'journalism.' The blogger owns his or her blog, is her own editor and publisher, accountable to no one else. But the blogger can also be a journalist writing in a journalistic style. There is room enough for both."

RAMONA GRIGG, WWW.RAMONASVOICES.BLOGSPOT.COM

"Professional doesn't have to mean corporate or impersonal."

BLOGGER STORY

"I do believe that a mark of a professional blog is when you start making money from it. Having said that, just because a blog is a money-earner, that alone doesn't make it professional, in that the content may not be high quality. You only have to look at a typical 'sponsored post' to see that it's little more than a company's About Us page copy-and-pasted. Some bloggers are so intent on making money that I think their content has become secondary: they've lost their voices."

SHAQINAH FAKAR, WWW.FBLSOCIETY.COM

#4 CHECK YOUR STATS REGULARLY

IT'S VITAL TO TRACK WHAT'S HAPPENING ON YOUR BLOG—HOW MANY VISITORS YOU'RE GETTING, NUMBERS OF COMMENTS, WHICH POSTS ARE THE MOST POPULAR, WHICH POSTS ARE ATTRACTING ATTENTION ON SOCIAL MEDIA, AND SO ON. THE GREAT THING ABOUT DIGITAL MEDIA IS THAT IT'S SO EASY TO MEASURE EVERYTHING, AND ALL BLOG SOFTWARE COMES WITH AT LEAST BASIC STATS. YOUR STATS TELL YOU WHAT'S WORKING AND WHAT ISN'T, AT A GLANCE.

Where it comes from:

In the world of work, we're told that the only goals worth having are those that are SMART: Specific, Measurable, Achievable, Relevant, and Timed—otherwise you're just kidding yourself, or worse, wasting your time. For example, a typical goal for a blogger might be "to increase the monthly number of unique visitors to my blog by 30% over the next six months." You could say this satisfies the SMART criteria. It certainly focuses you on what you're trying to achieve. Having a deadline is the element that's often forgotten, and yet it's probably the most crucial, because it means there is a definite date when you can ask yourself, "has this goal been achieved?" If the answer is no, it's a sign that something isn't working and needs changing.

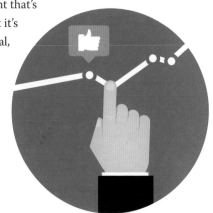

WHEN TO BREAK THE RULE

1. If you're not that interested.
Not all bloggers are motivated by fame and fortune. If the thought of growing an audience isn't on your agenda then you're unlikely to be poring over the stats. Some bloggers do it for fun, for their own satisfaction, for the fun of sharing what they love, for showcasing their creations, and expressing themselves. Whether they've picked up thirty new followers in a day or had their photos shared on Facebook is neither here nor there.

2. If you're not into competition.
Giving too much credence to statistics can encourage a win-or-lose mentality. If you're not competing with others, you're competing with yourself, and that can be just as stressful. Instead of telling you something useful, stats often throw up worrying questions (Why have visitor stats gone down? What was wrong with that post, since nobody commented?). Like the dieter stepping on the scales every day, watching the numbers can be an emotional rollercoaster ride that for some people takes away from the joy of blogging. Besides, numbers aren't the be all and end all. (*See also Rule #20.*)

3. If you're getting obsessed.
Remember, there is a difference between wanting to know if you've achieved a goal, and checking stats every day for the sake of it. Instead of worrying about every follower you lose or post that isn't performing as well as you expected, set yourself some SMART goals, and put your energy into something constructive.

RISK FACTOR: LOW

CHECK YOUR STATS REGULARLY

BLOGGER STORY

"It's true you can use Google Analytics to measure your blog traffic—many do. Other bloggers track how their readership is growing, and some like to talk about the number of Twitter followers or Facebook fans they have. I've heard of bloggers giving up altogether because they haven't been getting many comments or were worried that nobody was reading their blog. I think the most important thing is how you feel about your blog—your motivation for doing it in the first place. If you find something lacking, improve that component. Otherwise, if you're happy with your blog, it's successful! What more do you have to prove?"

MICHELLE MINNAAR, WWW.GREEDYGOURMET.COM

"If you're happy with your blog, it's successful! What more do you have to prove?"

MICHELLE MINNAAR

EXPERT COMMENT

"If you're a blogger, you've inevitably heard people mention various stats associated with their blogs. These include Google PageRank, Alexa Ranking, Page Authority, Compete Ranking, Klout Score, and the like. I won't get into what each of those stats mean and how they're calculated—that kind of info can be found with a simple Google search.

"The important thing to know is that you should be paying attention to these stats if you want your blog to grow. You don't need to know your current blog stats off the top of your head or check them religiously every single day. Some bloggers do stay on top of those stats to that degree, but you probably have more important work to do on your blog. Obviously, keeping tabs on stats is just a small part of the battle. The crucial part is that you find ways to improve all of those statistics. If you enjoy working with goals, it can become a bit of a game."

JEREMY BIBERDORF, WWW.MODESTMONEY.COM

POST SOMETHING EVERY DAY

THE RESEARCH ON THIS SEEMS UNEQUIVOCAL: THE MORE OFTEN YOU BLOG, THE MORE QUICKLY YOU GROW YOUR READERSHIP. IF IT'S IMPORTANT FOR YOU TO HAVE VISITORS, AND IF YOU WANT YOUR BLOG TO BECOME A HIVE OF DISCUSSION AND ACTIVITY, THEN YOU NEED TO POST EVERY DAY.

Where it comes from:
Pro bloggers have always recommended posting frequently. The reason is partly to do with search-engine rankings: search engines love fresh content, and the competition for appearing on the first page of Google is increasing all the time. If you post new content frequently, Google classes it as more current and relevant than a similar blog only updating once a month. Also, frequent posting will increase your overall visibility—you'll appear in subscribers' readers every day, get more retweets and mentions, shares and likes, and from there, more subscribers.

WHEN TO BREAK THE RULE

Some of the best blogs in the world post new content every day, sometimes several times a day. Most have staff bloggers and have more in common with traditional media than individual blogs. Huffington Post, Mashable, and CopyBlogger all started as the projects of individuals but grew to mass-media status. Nine or ten years ago when these pro blogs started out, there wasn't the competition, and high posting frequency won them huge audiences very quickly.

It's still the case that frequent posting has a positive effect on search-engine rankings. But quality is at least as important, particularly for human visitors (as opposed to search-engine robots), and pandering to the search engines can get out of hand. (*See also Rule #19.*)

You also need to consider the amount of time and effort needed to maintain this level of activity. It's better to start off posting at a frequency you can manage, then up the ante as and when you feel able or want to. If your posting schedule has you losing enthusiasm, you'll never keep your blog going. Find out what suits you. Seth Godin (sethgodin.typepad.com) is famous for blogging every day, but he never gives the impression it's a chore, or that the post has been "phoned in."

RISK FACTOR: LOW

#5 POST SOMETHING EVERY DAY

BLOGGER STORY

"I used to blog every day, and although it wasn't easy, it taught me many lessons:

"Don't underestimate the importance of a morning routine: creative people can struggle to get things done. Getting up early to blog did more for me than just improve my blogging. There's more inside of you than you think: the more you write, the more creative you become. As long as you're writing on something you're passionate about, you'll keep taking your writing to a new level the more you do it. See every moment as an opportunity to learn: when you blog every day, it makes you look for inspiration everywhere, from the conversations you have to the meals you eat. Don't fear criticism: publishing can be scary—how will others react to what you've written? But you can't allow this to control you. Otherwise, your ideas will stay in your head. Blogging has taught me this: don't fear criticism. Just keep creating.

"Although I no longer believe it's necessary to blog every day, I wholeheartedly believe in writing every day for the above reasons and more."

DAVID SANTISTEVAN, WWW.DAVIDSANTISTEVAN.COM

" EXPERT COMMENT

"I am not a fan of daily blogging, despite all the valid arguments in favor of it. Here's my case against churning out a new post every day:

- I am not a full-time writer. Small business owners have to wear many professional hats, and blogging is just one of mine.
- Sometimes I would rather read or watch TV or play tennis than write.
- I have other writing to do.
- More blog posts equals greater potential overlap. After a while, you just can't shake that feeling that you've seen that movie before.
- Less is more/the quality argument. A commitment to daily blogging can mean some posts aren't terribly good, original, or timely.

"If you want to put something out there every day or every hour, then knock yourself out. Before doing so, consider the drawbacks of a daily blogging strategy. You may find that the squeeze isn't worth the juice."

PHIL SIMON, WWW.PHILSIMON.COM

#6 SPELLING & GRAMMAR MISTAKES WILL KILL YOUR BLOG

THE RULE

IF YOU WANT YOUR BLOG TO BE TAKEN SERIOUSLY AND ARE HOPING TO ATTRACT NEW SUBSCRIBERS, IT'S ESSENTIAL TO PROOFREAD FOR SPELLING AND GRAMMATICAL ERRORS. SPELLING MISTAKES SCREAM "SLOPPY!" AND YOU WILL LOSE CREDIBILITY AND READERS.

Where it comes from:

Would you be proud of sending a business letter or submitting a book proposal with spelling errors? If you were going for your dream job, would you be happy submitting a resumé full of mistakes? Probably not—and that's the basis of this rule. We are judged by the quality of our presentation, and that includes how we present ourselves in writing. Poor spelling can undermine a blogger's credibility, especially on a business blog or one that aspires to professionalism (*see also Rule #3*). Blogging experts are pretty much united on this one, so surely there are no grounds to break it?

WHEN TO BREAK THE RULE

Blogging is a peculiar form of writing. More informal than a business letter, but not as casual as a text. Conversational, but without the false starts, the ums and ahs, and the natural rhythms of speech. Published, but with less permanence than a printed document.

Perfect spelling, correct vocabulary, and logical sentence structure all contribute to good, clear communication. But blogging is also about timeliness; about seizing the moment and letting the words flow; about getting across your personality as well as your ideas. If you find yourself constantly worrying that your grammar isn't technically perfect, or re-writing over and over until you can hardly bear to hit "publish," your blog post may lose its conversational tone. Worse still, blogging will start to feel like hard work and a time suck.

It's also good to remember that a blog post can be edited after it's published. Some people might still spot the errors before you've had a chance to correct them, but at least you can put the record straight at any time—it's not completely out of your hands like a printed book is!

Unless you're a grammar guru telling people how to write, you will probably get away with a bit of "creative" language use. In some cases it can even be charming. If what you're sharing on your blog is of interest to the reader, they will keep reading and will be relatively forgiving of typos and dangling participles.

RISK FACTOR: MEDIUM TO HIGH

#6 SPELLING & GRAMMAR MISTAKES WILL KILL YOUR BLOG

EXPERT COMMENT

"You may find it amusing to know that I, like David Ogilvy, have never learned the formal rules of grammar. I learned to write by reading obsessively at an early age, but when it came time to learn the 'rules', I tuned out. If you show me an incorrect sentence, I can fix it, but if I need to know the technical reason why it was wrong in the first place, I go ask my wife."

BRIAN CLARK, WWW.COPYBLOGGER.COM

"The fewer grammar or misspellings you have, the more likely someone will enjoy your phenomenal blog post."

MELISSA CULBERTSON, WWW.BLOGCLARITY.COM

BLOGGER STORY

"If like me you tend to write quickly, you're trying to get your ideas on the page while they're in your head, and I can't do that when I'm stopping midthoughtwise to ponder whether there's a comma here or this participle is dangling or there is no such word as 'midthoughtwise.'

"In scriptwriting, you see this in rewrite sessions. Someone pitches a joke, everyone laughs, the assistant starts transcribing it, and there's always one person barking out that there should be a comma there, or that's a semicolon. Let whoever proofs the script deal with that. Don't slow down the process by blurting out that 'dad' needs to be capitalized.

"The point is, from time to time (on my blog) you will see grammatical mistakes, misspelled words, made up words, tenses changing, inconsistencies, italics for no reason, and other egregious clerical errors. I do try to proof these posts, but things still slip by. So I beg your indulgence. I don't have an editor."

KEN LEVINE, KENLEVINE.BLOGSPOT.COM

#7 KEEP BLOG POSTS SHORT

KEEP BLOG POSTS SHORT (UNDER 500 WORDS IS A TYPICAL GUIDELINE) BECAUSE PEOPLE HAVE SHORT ATTENTION SPANS, ESPECIALLY WHEN READING ON THE WEB, AND ARE PUSHED FOR TIME. IF YOU REALLY WANT TO POST LONG ARTICLES, THEN BREAK THEM DOWN INTO EPISODES AND POST THEM AS TWO- OR THREE-PARTERS.

Where it comes from:
A few years ago, reading a lot of text on a screen was considered hard work, so long articles were frowned upon and bloggers were advised to present their copy in easily-scannable chunks. Short posts were also favored by the post-every-day brigade, for obvious reasons. The advice was to post short, post more frequently, break it up with visual content, get your main points over quickly, and not test people's patience.

Now, however, there are some strong arguments for questioning this rule. Thanks to the proliferation of tablets and e-readers, we're now very used to reading on-screen. Some topics benefit from a more reflective and in-depth treatment. Longer posts are often seen as offering greater value, and are subsequently more often shared, favorited, and commented on. Plus, longer blog posts can rank better in searches.

WHEN TO BREAK THE RULE

First of all, be guided by your subject matter and your audience. The focus of a fashion or design blog will be great photos and visual imagery. A blog post might consist of a large number of photos but not necessarily many words. But sometimes a high word count is appropriate. A business blogger may wish to demonstrate authority through how-to articles, with a view to being found on Google. In this case, longer blog posts would do a better job. A book blogger might want to write in-depth reviews of new books, or interviews. A short post is unlikely to do justice to the subject.

Your next consideration ought to be your own blogging style— are you a fast writer, able to get something up and out quickly? Or do you like to get it right, even if that means spending hours on it and only hitting the "publish" button when you're absolutely happy with what you've written? Your blog should be sustainable. If you're likely to spend too long on each blog post you'll end up posting very infrequently, so "keep it short" might be a good maxim.

In reality, it's fine to produce both short and long posts, and readers may actually appreciate the variety. If you're concerned, you can always experiment to find out what works best for you and your blog.

RISK FACTOR: LOW

#7 KEEP BLOG POSTS SHORT

EXPERT COMMENT

"Google's Panda update punishes websites with thin content, or pages full of links or search-engine optimization (SEO) writing. If your average article length is under 200 words, search engines will likely be more critical of the content, and the general rule of thumb is that articles of 300 words or more are less likely to put you at risk for infringing on 'thin' content.

"However, this is your online presence, not your 9th grade English essay. Bloggers that write just to hit a word count will get the same results as when you wrote a summary about *Romeo and Juliet* in summer school: a C+ grade at best.

"Before the age of the internet, writers advised to avoid using five words when one would suffice. That phrase rings true today. There's a difference between short content and thin content. Thin content is chock-full of keywords, low in quality, and rehashed from other sites. Short content is original and concise, and offers value to readers, not search engines."

DAVID SNYDER, WWW.COPYPRESS.COM

"I don't write long posts for the sake of writing long posts. I need length and context to get my point across. I used to write short blog posts. I also blogged for over a year and racked up a massive 17 blog subscribers. These days I feel 'wrong' if I write anything less than 2,000 words. That's not because I have to, but because the message I want to get across takes at least that much writing.

"At the end of the day, short writing is easy (for the most part; Seth Godin is a good exception). Writing long articles that hold interest is hard, but the payoff is well worth it. My longer blog posts get shared and read and commented on more than any other blogger I see writing short posts. That's the biggest signal I need."

GLEN ALLSOPP, WWW.VIPERCHILL.COM

"There's a difference between short content and thin content."

DAVID SNYDER

#8 STICK TO ONE TOPIC OR NICHE

YOU SHOULD BLOG ABOUT A SPECIFIC SUBJECT, AND NOT GO OFF-TOPIC.

Blogging about cupcakes? Then nobody cares what you think about the latest Broadway show. Nor do they want to read about the minutiae of your private life. The reason you've built a readership for your blog is that you know cupcakes—how to make them, where to buy them, who eats them, what makes a prize-winning cupcake, and so on. If you start reviewing musicals out of the blue, your blog will be a ghost town before you can say *"Phantom of the Opera."*

Where it comes from:
As with many blogging rules, this one is straight out of the business studies textbook. We are constantly bombarded with marketing messages, to the point that we're blind to most of them. If you want to be noticed in business, you have to be very clear who you're talking to and what interests them—in other words, everything you say has to be relevant to those you want to reach. Prove your relevance, and your audience will eventually become your best ambassadors.

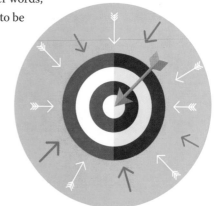

WHEN TO BREAK THE RULE

This rule gets broken all the time, but to do so successfully you need to have built up a little blogging karma. When starting a blog from scratch, settling on a topic and sticking with it is a pretty good strategy. But you may well find your staunchest followers grow to like your style, your insights, your opinions… and if you want to stray from your niche from time to time, they'll enjoy the experience as much as you.

Going off-topic doesn't necessarily mean a complete change. It could also be that you want to expand your blogging niche to suit your growing interests. Maybe you started off blogging about cupcakes, but you start writing the odd post to do with baking generally. This is a good way of testing a new niche or topic. See how your readers respond. Even if you lose some readers, you may gain others.

Conversely, you might start writing on a broad blog topic, such as photography, but over time decide you're really only interested in blogging about wildlife photography.

But there are alternatives—you could write the occasional guest post on another blog, if you feel the topic is not a good fit with yours. Or you could even start another blog—who knows, the second blog could take off and become your primary home on the web.

RISK FACTOR: LOW TO MEDIUM

!

#8 STICK TO ONE TOPIC OR NICHE

 **BLOGGER STORY**

"Writing with a niche in mind has given me nothing but headaches. I end up feeling stifled and unable to open up. Grechen Reiter (of Grechen's Closet, (grechenscloset.com) excels at it amazingly; when I go to her site, I know exactly what stores, designers, and brands to expect. And I trust her because of it.

"Rather than a niche, it's better for me to think of my blog as a place to share curiosity, knowledge, and discovery. It keeps me enthused. If a niche keeps you energized, stick with it. If it doesn't work for you, don't feel bad about it or spend time worrying about it. Just do what inspires you and makes you happy."

ASHLEY ROBISON, INDEPENDENT FASHION BLOGGERS, WWW.HEARTIFB.COM

"Writing with a niche in mind has given me nothing but headaches."

ASHLEY ROBISON

BLOGGER STORY

"When beginning my blog, A Perfect Gray, I wanted to distinguish my 'blog voice' in some way. There are many decor and design blogs on the web, so I decided to capitalize on my love of neutral interiors, and especially my love of the color gray—the 'new neutral' in the decorating world.

"I really didn't appreciate what a huge trend the color gray would become, and would continue to be, in the decor world. Now I find that my blog posts featuring gray colors, rooms, and furniture are my most popular posts, some receiving over 100,000 views.

"I definitely try to stick to my 'gray' theme. I consider my blog an 'inspiration' blog, and my readers count on coming to my site for continued inspiration for their own spaces. Not that I don't throw in an occasional, off-topic post, because I do! Fun, quirky, and different posts are always well received, but I do keep them to a minimum. The topic that I always stick to is home decor."

DONNA PEAY, A PERFECT GRAY,
WWW.APERFECTGRAY.COM

#9 ALWAYS END WITH A QUESTION

IF YOU WANT PEOPLE TO COMMENT ON YOUR BLOG THEN YOU SHOULD END EACH BLOG POST WITH A QUESTION. PEOPLE BASICALLY NEED PROMPTING WHEN IT COMES TO TAKING ACTION, AND IF YOU DON'T ASK, YOU DON'T GET.

Where it comes from:
This rule refers to a classic element of direct marketing—the call to action. When people are asked or told to do something, they tend to respond; when you're asked a direct question it's hard to resist answering, especially if the question is deliberately provocative. Obviously, the question has to be related to what's gone before, not just a random quiz question. The question may be accompanied by an instruction or command to comment, just to make it clear what you want. So for example, if you've written an opinion piece about music education, you might end with "Do you think XYZ was right to decrease funding for music in schools? Tell me what you think in the comments." The direct marketer would favor a sales-related question or command: "Want to know more about SEO for florists? Buy my book now!"

> "From a retention and recall view, middles suck. Endings are crucial. They're what sticks."
>
> **KATHY SIERRA**

WHEN TO BREAK THE RULE

Like many of the rules, there's nothing wrong with this one, but it is a simplification. You may well have asked questions during the course of the blog post, and if they were engaging enough, then readers may well be moved to respond. The topic itself may already be controversial, which will increase the likelihood of comments. The sales-related question might be appropriate on a business blog, but not at the end of every post, otherwise readers will start to think your blog is just one fat not-very-subtly-disguised advertisement.

Most bloggers agree that a post shouldn't just tail off. You don't have to end on a witty flourish, but a strong ending can mean many things, and it doesn't have to be a question. It could just be a one-line conclusion or summary of key points. Or a link to a related post, interview, or product. If you've written a how-to post, you could end with an assignment or "three things you can do now," for example. A sales pitch is fine, but try to vary it—and think of it as a nudge, rather than a push.

RISK FACTOR: MEDIUM

#9   ALWAYS END WITH A QUESTION

EXPERT COMMENT

"We can all take a lesson from film-makers: endings matter. The way we end a conversation, blog post, presentation, song, whatever…is what they'll remember most. The end can matter more to readers than everything we did before. And the feeling they leave with is the one they might have forever.

"It's not just film-makers that appreciate The End— learning theory has known this for a long time. Students in a classroom are more likely to remember what they learned/heard/did first and last than whatever happened in the middle. From a retention and recall view, middles suck. Endings are crucial. They're what sticks."

KATHY SIERRA, SERIOUSPONY.COM

EXPERT COMMENT

"Ending a blog post with a question is one good way to do it, but it's not the only one. A relevant link or links can also work—there are plenty of WordPress plug-ins that can create an auto-generated list of related posts, for example. If your post features a project or something readers could try for themselves, you could offer one or two specific action points, such as 'Choose one of these recipes to try this weekend.' You might end a post with an embedded email sign-up box and a few words about why they should sign up for it. Alternatively, sometimes a simple but strong summary is appropriate, especially if it has been a lengthy or complex post—and it's a good way to make sure you leave readers feeling confident about what they've just read."

ALI LUKE, ZENOPTIMISE.COM

#10 BLOG ABOUT YOUR TOPIC, NOT ABOUT YOURSELF

PEOPLE VISIT YOUR BLOG BECAUSE THEY'RE INTERESTED IN THE SUBJECT MATTER; THEY'RE NOT THERE TO HANG OUT.

Whether you're blogging about books, movies, or garden design, what you have is a blog, not a social network. This means you should keep all those status updates about your kids, your pets, and your digestive system to yourself. Facebook is perfect for that kind of chat. You may even belong to a super-friendly online forum devoted to something specific, such as Malaysian cuisine or historic re-enactments of battles, but where off-topic chat is welcome.

Where it comes from:
It's partly a rebuke often aimed at hobby bloggers by those who would like blogging to be taken more seriously, or by those who have little time for the "time-wasting" chitchat of social networks. The argument goes something along the lines of "If I subscribe to a blog about self-build cabins, I want to read about how to get started, or look at some cabin inspiration; I don't want to hear about the blogger's impending divorce."

There have always been concerns with the internet and privacy, and that's another good reason for not talking too freely about your private life. As with most of the "rules," this one incites strong opinions on both sides.

WHEN TO BREAK THE RULE

This rule is often broken and it's really your choice and no one else's. For many bloggers, it's a case of trial and error. You will be swayed firstly by your own communication preferences and personality. If you're already a social sharer, this could easily spill over into your blog. If you're naturally reserved, you may balk at the idea of writing in a conversational style, let alone sharing personal details with your readers.

The other things to consider are the subject matter (some blog topics lend themselves naturally to talk about home life or family) and how you want your blog to be perceived—journalistic? Instructional? Cutting edge? Business oriented?

Do people really want to hear about your hospital appointments or your children going off to university? Writing about your personal life may feel inappropriate. But some bloggers have found that sharing something real and personal with readers has given them a new and more powerful connection. A blog written by an individual is usually a far more personal form of publishing than you find in traditional media (this is less true of group or magazine-style blogs). This can be something to celebrate.

RISK FACTOR: LOW TO MEDIUM

#10 BLOG ABOUT YOUR TOPIC, NOT ABOUT YOURSELF

 **BLOGGER STORY**

There are times when real life gets too important to ignore, and when a blogger not known for oversharing brings up one of life's big issues, it can have a far-reaching effect.

Danny Brown is a well-known social media blogger and online marketing expert. He is a business blogger. Then one day he took his readers by surprise, by sharing a story about his grandparents, about loss, about a life lesson he had learned. It was a brief post, but the comments poured in.

Judy Lee Dunn recalls how she read this post just days after her own father died, and she realized that "when bloggers do stray from their topic, even write an emotional post, that is precisely when I connect with them—and on a much deeper level. Because they have let me inside."

JUDY LEE DUNN, JUDYLEEDUNN.COM

BLOGGER STORY

"How much of yourself should you share on your blog? There's no right or wrong way to go about it. My take? No matter who you are, the most important thing is to develop your blog's voice. So if you're comfortable telling stories about your personal life or sharing your opinion about hot button topics, go for it.

"But, if you're not game to put your personal life on the internet, you shouldn't feel obligated to do so—there are plenty of other ways to develop your blog's voice (think: useful, original content, a unique photographic style, or injecting humor—the list really goes on).

"In my own experience, I've found that posts that share insights into my personal life often get the highest levels of engagement. But beyond the stats, for me, the best part is hearing from other women and either realizing I'm not alone in whatever I'm struggling with, or realizing that something I've written might have helped someone, even just a little bit. That is so gratifying—to me, it's really what the whole 'blogging community' is about!"

VICTORIA MCGINLEY, WWW.SHOPTHEBBAR.COM

#11 DON'T BE ANONYMOUS

SHOW YOUR FACE RATHER THAN HIDING BEHIND AN ANONYMOUS NAME OR AVATAR. A BLOG IS A PERSONAL TYPE OF WEBSITE, AND READERS WANT TO KNOW THE PERSON BEHIND IT. IF THERE'S NO NAME TO BE FOUND, AND IF YOU MAKE IT DIFFICULT FOR READERS TO CONTACT YOU, VISITORS WILL BE PUT OFF AND YOU'LL MISS OUT ON OPPORTUNITIES.

Where it comes from:
Before the internet was commercialized—say, up to the mid- to late-1990s, there were far fewer people online and there was a kind of Wild West mentality. Bulletin boards (the forerunners to today's social networks) could erupt into vicious arguments. Not surprisingly, newcomers to this scene were cautious, and for a while it was the norm to use made-up names and avatars. It didn't make people entirely untraceable, just less obviously who they were "in real life."

In the online world we know today, however, true anonymity tends to be associated with illegal activities, scamming, spamming, and the "dark web." Social networks encourage, even require members to use their real names, and as a result it's now less common for people to adopt pseudonyms. A blog is a person's home territory, so it should be a safe place to be yourself.

Experts have been saying for a while now that if you're concerned with building relationships of trust online (which businesses certainly are) then your presence needs to be authentic and open, because only crooks hide their identity. By showing your name and face, you're distancing yourself from those who have good reason to stay anonymous.

WHEN TO BREAK THE RULE

There is a big problem with this rule—it assumes the only reason to stay anonymous is a sinister one. But what about citizen-journalists, political commentators or activists, whistle-blowers, or people in sensitive jobs where confidentiality is paramount?

Clearly, a blogger isn't going to embrace full transparency if it will put themself, their job, or their family seriously at risk. Bloggers have always argued for the right to remain anonymous and that the whole point of blogging is to allow your voice to be heard, without censorship by the powers that be.

But let's say you don't fall into the above category of blogger. Maybe you're blogging to build your career prospects, or about an activity you really love, or just for fun. Maybe you're blogging in support of a business or as a start of something new. Do you have a valid reason to stay anonymous or are you just a bit shy? If it's the latter, try to get over it. There is virtually no benefit to being a person of mystery if the only excuse you have is that you don't like having your photo taken. On the other hand, if wearing a mask is crucial to your art or style, go right ahead and make a feature of it, as some bloggers have done.

RISK FACTOR: MEDIUM TO HIGH

#11   DON'T BE ANONYMOUS

EXPERT COMMENT

"The reason you're blogging is the opposite of anonymity. You want people to be able to put your name (or pen name) into a search engine and find you. Don't make them rummage in their memory banks trying to remember if your blog is called 'Songs from the Zombiepocalypse', or 'Lost Marbles'. A whole lot more people will find you if they can just Google 'Your Name'.

"Every minute you spend blogging anonymously is a minute wasted. Let the public know who you are and where you are and why we should be reading your stuff, instead of the other ten billion blogs out there.

"And ALWAYS put your contact information prominently on the blog. If you're selling a product, it's just plain dumb not to tell people where to find it."

ANNE R. ALLEN, ANNERALLEN.BLOGSPOT.COM

11

BLOGGER STORY

"I started my blog in August of 2011 as a way to share as much about my life as I could so that I could improve what was going on. I figured the best way to do this was to blog anonymously because I could be completely honest about everything (my dad had recently passed away at this point in my life and there were major things going wrong in my life due to that) without any repercussions.

"I decided to change my mind when I realized that I was holding myself back by being anonymous. I knew I wanted to take blogging to the next level, and it was hard to do that if I was anonymous. I knew my business needed a face."

MICHELLE SCHROEDER,
WWW.MAKINGSENSEOFCENTS.COM

"Every minute you spend blogging anonymously is a minute wasted."

ANNE R. ALLEN

#12 ALWAYS INCLUDE AT LEAST ONE IMAGE

EVERY BLOG POST SHOULD INCLUDE AT LEAST ONE IMAGE—IMAGES MAKE A BLOG MORE READABLE, ATTRACTIVE, AND UNIQUE. THEY BREAK UP THE TEXT TO KEEP THE READER'S INTEREST, THEY CAN ILLUSTRATE OR MAKE A POINT MORE SUCCINCTLY THAN MERE WORDS, THEY CAN ENTERTAIN, OR THEY CAN SET THE MOOD.

Where it comes from:
The web is a visual medium, and studies have shown that people's attention is drawn more by images than by words. So images will make your blog easier on the eye and more "sticky"; people will stay longer and come back more often. Not only that, but people love sharing images via social media—not just photos but also videos, illustrations, and infographics. Each time you post an image you're creating another opportunity for visitors to share your content with their social networks, bringing fame and possibly fortune for your blog.

The popularity of digital photo sharing has been steadily growing from the early days of Flickr through phone apps such as Instagram, blogging platforms such as Tumblr, and image-sharing social networks such as Pinterest. It's not going away any time soon.

WHEN TO BREAK THE RULE

What are you blogging about? If you're a creative person, if yours is a photo blog, if you have an eye for color and design, I am obviously preaching to the converted, and images may well be the cornerstone of your blog already. But for many business bloggers, journalists, writers, or academics, this rule might seem unimportant. Worse still, it can become a burden.

We have all seen business blogs posting generic images of office staff or computer keyboards. Royalty-free photography sites can often come to the rescue when you need an appropriate image. But the key word here is *appropriate*. It is a mistake to resort to clip art or cheesy-looking stock images simply because you're trying to obey this rule.

If the subject of your blog doesn't have an obvious visual angle (perhaps it's about grammar advice, or vacuum pumps, or patents law…), don't worry about shoehorning an image into every post. Better to hold off until you have a truly relevant photo or video to share, and it will have more impact on your readers.

RISK FACTOR: MEDIUM

#12 ALWAYS INCLUDE AT LEAST ONE IMAGE

BLOGGER STORY

"When I read blogs, my eyes usually skip over the image to focus on the text. I'm a writer and an avid reader. I think in words. Therefore, it didn't occur to me to use images on my blog. My blog has a steadily growing base of subscribers, gets referenced on book covers and publishers' promotional material, and attracts social media links, despite the lack of images.

"When I write a blog article I do use short paragraphs, bold headings for key information, and bullet points, so they are visually easy to look at without needing an image to 'break up the text.' The only time I have used an image to provide a break in the text was for a four-thousand-word film review.

"A relevant image can enhance a blog article, but a clichéd stock image can deter readers, so I focus on making the text as visually appealing as possible."

EMMA LEE, WWW.EMMALEE1.WORDPRESS.COM

BLOGGER STORY

"I think you're more likely to purchase a magazine with an eye-catching cover photo than one with no cover photo at all. The image is what grabs your attention. Blogs are no different. As bloggers, we are storytellers, and we use images to help us tell the story. The subject matter of my blog, Bright Bold & Beautiful, is very visual—art, design, and interiors—and one way I make it stand out is to include striking, original photos in every post. It's a busy, popular blog. If you're taking your own photos, the most important elements are light (use natural light whenever possible) and composition (frame the subject and get up close). There are so many good, free photo-editing tools out there—experiment and have fun."

LAURA TREVEY, WWW.BRIGHTBOLDBEAUTIFUL.COM

"A clichéd, stock image can deter readers."

EMMA LEE

#13 AVOID LIGHT TEXT ON A DARK BACKGROUND

LIGHT-COLORED TEXT ON A DARK BACKGROUND, ESPECIALLY ON A SCREEN, IS DIFFICULT TO READ, SO IT'S ALWAYS ADVISABLE TO GO FOR A LIGHT BACKGROUND AND DARK TEXT.

Where it comes from:

There are some design and usability rules that date right back to the late 1990s, long before blogging took off. In principle, many of them still apply—not just to blogs, but to websites generally. It really comes down to consideration for your audience. Everyone has their pet peeves about what they like or don't like on websites, but if you literally *can't read it*, then you're probably not coming back. The rule is not "black-on-white only" but you do need a strong contrast between the text and the background. Size also matters—although these days it's quite easy to magnify the screen, you don't always want to zoom in and lose the big picture.

"Know when it's appropriate to use a dark design based on your content and target audience."

KAYLA KNIGHT

WHEN TO BREAK THE RULE

Dark backgrounds are commonly associated with certain types of content. Authors in the fantasy or horror genres love them. They can often be found on blogs by or for teenagers and gamers, or on subjects like cars, photography, technology, or web design. A search for "dark blog themes" brings up a feast of options. So white-on-black is very much alive and kicking. But if you're going to break this rule, you need a good reason, and you should also be confident that your audience won't find it a turn-off.

A black background has its functions—on-screen, it can certainly make colors pop more dramatically than against a white or pale background. If you're desperate for a dark look, all is not lost. Maybe you're writing nice short blog posts, or you're breaking up your copy into one-sentence paragraphs. Perhaps your blog is visuals-led, with simple captions. You can mitigate your readers' eyestrain by using a clear, sans-serif typeface like Verdana, in a good size, with generous line spacing. Or perhaps your audience is young and/or hip enough not to be bothered by boring stuff like eyestrain. Your call!

RISK FACTOR: MEDIUM TO HIGH

#13 AVOID LIGHT TEXT ON A DARK BACKGROUND

 **EXPERT COMMENT**

"Gray type is a design fad these days. It's thought to look tasteful. And if you use it, you are choosing to have your copy less read and less comprehended.

"And guess what: every color other than black is hard to read in text sizes. If you want people to read what you've written, use black type. And while you're thinking about readability, put that black type over a white background—any background tint that's darker than 5% seriously impedes readability.

"This is unpopular advice among brand shamans and some designers. But if people are going to respond in some specific way (like giving a gift), they're going to need to be motivated in a specific way, through specific actual words they can read. Good design supports that motivation because of the way it feels. But you've defeated yourself if the design makes the copy unreadable.

"So lose the gray. And the blue. And all those other tasteful, brand-mandated text colors. Go with black."

JEFF BROOKS, WWW.FUTUREFUNDRAISINGNOW.COM

" EXPERT COMMENT

"Dark websites can be beautiful. They also pose a threat of less readability, eyestrain, and lost content, so their lighter counterparts are often preferred.

"When designing a dark website—for the benefit of everyone—take some of the essential aesthetics into consideration! Use more space around elements and within copy, but particularly between site sections for hierarchy. Use taller line heights and bigger fonts, and avoid serif fonts, unless for headlines or text otherwise large enough to be clear. Don't use straight black and white, but rather darker and lighter grays to ease eyestrain, and, if applicable, choose simple color palettes to complement the design.

"Most importantly: know when it's appropriate to use a dark web design, based on the content and target audience. A great idea also is to create a usable style switcher that can swap out a darker website for a lighter version—great for those who prefer lighter website reading or otherwise have accessibility issues."

KAYLA KNIGHT, WWW.KAYLAKNIGHT.COM

#14 KILLER HEADLINES ARE ESSENTIAL

THE HEADLINE OR TITLE OF YOUR BLOG POST IS A CRUCIAL ELEMENT TO GET RIGHT. SUCCESSFUL BLOGGERS ALWAYS SPEND TIME AND EFFORT ON THIS BECAUSE KILLER HEADLINES ATTRACT VISITORS TO YOUR BLOG. IF YOU DON'T PAY ATTENTION TO THIS RULE, YOUR VISITOR NUMBERS WILL SUFFER, PLAIN AND SIMPLE.

Where it comes from:
Right from the first days of the printing press, poster makers and pamphlet publishers experimented with different typefaces, placement, and wording in their quest to catch people's attention. Even now, newspapers recognize the importance of headlines, and the job of writing them is a specialist one, not left to the likes of the lowly reporter. The digital publishing explosion has meant we are now faced with an avalanche of media shouting for our attention. As consumers of this media, we have to be choosy. Even reading a headline is time-consuming, so if that doesn't grab you, the rest of the article is unlikely even to get a glance. In a headline, *every word counts*.

There's a whole branch of blog psychology that deals purely with headlines. Pro bloggers talk about the use of "power words" (words that trigger something in our minds and pull us in). They know that a small tweak can make the difference between a sky-high click-through rate and a blog post that sinks without a trace. Simply put, they've had many years of practice, and they've discovered what works and what doesn't. Ignore this advice at your peril.

WHEN TO BREAK THE RULE

First, here's when NOT to break it: when your blog needs to pay its way. If your ultimate reason for blogging is to make money, then you can't afford to dash off any old headline. A great headline creates a compelling reason to read on, through its newsworthiness, immediacy, relevance, entertainment value, or all of these factors. There are winning formulas, such as the familiar "How to avoid..." or "74 tips for..." (a random number such as 74 can standout more than 10 or 100, apparently).

But you can go too far—by making your headline too cute, or misleading. You'll get the click-throughs, but some readers will feel cheated. Overusing power words can get irritating. As a status update, a killer headline can come across as very sales-y.

If you're not on a sales mission, you might very well break this rule. If you're not hung up on the numbers, or if you are less interested in monetizing your blog and more interested in carrying on a conversation with like-minded people or simply sharing your views and ideas, you can probably take your foot off the power-word pedal. As long as your headlines are relevant, succinct, and not misleading, and as long as you are active in the same social spaces as your target readers, there is still a good chance your post will be seen, read, and shared. Your audience will probably grow organically over time, but you won't be giving up the day job.

RISK FACTOR: HIGH

KILLER HEADLINES ARE ESSENTIAL

"An attention-grabbing headline is the most important element of every blog post or article. I've seen so many business blog posts with super-boring headlines such as 'XYZ Case Study' or 'IT Tips.' If you're one of them, please stop wasting time here. Remember that the words you use in your headline/title are probably the most important words out of your entire blog post. Don't take my word for it. Here's what advertising guru David Ogilvy said: 'On average, five times as many people read the headline as read the body copy. When you have written your headline, you have spent eighty cents out of your dollar.'"

KOOZAI, WWW.KOOZAI.COM

"The goal of your headline is to stop readers cold and draw them into your post."

NEIL PATEL

EXPERT COMMENT

"The goal of the headline is to stop readers cold and draw them into your post. You can't do that if you use cute, clever, or confusing headlines. You can stop readers cold, however, if you write headlines that are unique, ultra-specific, useful, or urgent."

NEIL PATEL, WWW.QUICKSPROUT.COM

EXPERT COMMENT

"Readers tend to absorb the first three words of a headline and the last three words. These numbers via KISSmetrics come straight from usability research, revealing that we don't just scan body copy—we scan headlines, too.

"Of course, few headlines will be six words long in total. In those cases, it's important to make the first three words and the last three words stand out as much as possible."

KEVAN LEE, BUFFERAPP.COM

#15 PUBLICIZE YOUR BLOG POSTS ON SOCIAL MEDIA

THE RULE

THIS IS THE SOCIAL WEB, AND IT'S FUELED BY SHARES, LIKES, COMMENTS...AND LINKS. WHEN YOU WRITE A BLOG POST, YOU WANT AS MANY PEOPLE AS POSSIBLE TO SEE IT, BUT THAT'S NOT GOING TO HAPPEN UNLESS YOU PROMOTE, PROMOTE, PROMOTE (THAT'S TO SAY, POST A LINK TO IT) ON AS MANY DIFFERENT PLATFORMS AS POSSIBLE. THAT WAY, THERE'S A MUCH GREATER CHANCE THAT YOUR BLOG POST WILL GET READ AND NOTICED BY A LARGER NUMBER OF PEOPLE, ALL OF WHOM MAY THEN SHARE IT WITH THEIR FRIENDS. AND PUBLICIZING YOUR BLOG POSTS ACROSS THE BOARD IS EASY; THERE ARE EVEN TOOLS TO AUTOMATE THE PROCESS.

Where it comes from:
The idea of "spray and pray" has been around as long as marketing itself. With digital content, it's cheap, easy, and quick to promote something, so that's exactly what everyone does in the belief that it's just a numbers game: the more people who see your message, the better. And social media encourages the view that we are all now hyperconnected, which means every "share" has the potential to go viral. It's also easy to schedule updates in advance, which means that you can repeat the same messages many times, at different times of day. Result!

WHEN TO BREAK THE RULE

Of course you want to build your audience and draw people's attention to your blog, but trying to reach everybody by any means possible could simply backfire. Social media is not like traditional twentieth-century marketing channels. Treating it that way is risky. Yes, technology makes it easy to cross-post everywhere, but that's a crude strategy.

First of all, think about your friends and followers. Will they be interested enough to share or forward your update with their networks? Do you give generously to your network and share other people's updates and links? If so, people are more likely to reciprocate. (But only if your content is good!) If you only ever promote your own messages, you're more likely to annoy people.

Social networks are not a one-size-fits-all. You may have very different conversations and share different things on Pinterest than on LinkedIn, for example. And you connect there at different times of day, for different reasons.

Not everyone in your network will see your update. Of those who do, not all will share it, and not all of them will share it with all of their network. In other words, unless your update has instant, wide appeal, it's very unlikely to be shared much at all. It's important to realize this, because if you over-promote your blog posts there's a real risk you will irritate people enough for them to unfriend or unfollow you or your blog. The exposure you gain may not be worth the cost.

RISK FACTOR: MEDIUM

#15 PUBLICIZE YOUR BLOG POSTS ON SOCIAL MEDIA

BLOGGER STORY

"If your Twitter feed and Facebook wall are filled with updates on your latest blog post, your latest sale, your latest product, there is no real point in your even having a Twitter or a Facebook account.

"If you want your social media strategy to do what it's supposed to do (namely, engage and connect with readers), you need to follow the 80/20 rule—make sure that 80% of your updates are about things not related to you, you, you. They can be retweets of posts by other bloggers you love, inspirational quotes, links to news you think your readers will find valuable, questions to generate conversation. Only 20% of your updates should be self-promotional if you want to give people a reason to follow you."

KELLY GURNETT, WWW.CORDELIACALLSITQUITS.COM

EXPERT COMMENT

"If you're engaged with your followers and add value to your community, people are more likely to click on a link to your blog. But don't join every social network out there just so you can post links. That's likely to be a waste of time and may even lose you readers."

SAMANTHA MACARTHUR, WWW.FORTY-FIRST.CO.UK

"If you want your social media strategy to do what it's supposed to do, you need to follow the 80/20 rule."

KELLY GURNETT

#16 COMMENT REGULARLY ON OTHER BLOGS

A BLOGGER SHOULD MAKE A POINT OF COMMENTING REGULARLY ON OTHER PEOPLE'S BLOGS. NOT ONLY IS IT A WAY INTO CONVERSATIONS, IT WILL GET YOU NOTICED AND LEAD READERS TO YOUR BLOG.

Where it comes from:
In the early days of blogging, commenting was the only public way to join the conversation. Blogs with high numbers of comments were considered the most influential and authoritative, because comments were evidence of how many people were actively engaging with the blog content. Newbie bloggers realized that by leaving good quality comments on bigger, busier blogs, they stood a chance of being noticed and maybe even invited to write a guest post or two. The strategy was to leave a relevant comment plus your name and a link to your own blog. The link was important—not just for the host blogger and his or her readers to see, but also for those busy search engine spiders that would follow the link to your blog and benefit your search ranking.

Sadly, it was just too tempting for the spammers, and so links on blog comments are now invariably "nofollow"—meaning that search engine spiders will not hop over to the commenter's blog. As for the idea that leaving a comment on a Problogger post will lead to a phone call from Darren Rowse, those days are well and truly over. Not only that, but since the advent of social networks, much of the discussion that used to take place on blogs now happens on Facebook, Twitter, Google+, or LinkedIn.

WHEN TO BREAK THE RULE

Comments still have a place, and conversations still take place on blogs. Not everyone has decamped to Facebook. But the blogosphere is a big, diverse place. The top blogs are now pretty much online empires—very different animals to the individual, personal blogs that make up the majority of the blogosphere. While Copyblogger made the decision to remove comments entirely, most small-scale bloggers still encourage them and still want to read and comment on other blogs.

But commenting needs to be done for the right reasons. Don't comment on other blogs just to get attention or links to your blog, or to fulfill some "comment quota." It's not wise to leave drive-by comments like "Great post!" unless you want to be taken for a spammer.

On the other hand, reading other blogs and connecting with bloggers is one of the joys of blogging, and it can transform you from solitary blogger to a connected and connecting person online. Do leave thoughtful, relevant comments if you have something to add to the conversation. Or if you have an insightful post on a similar topic, then go ahead and share it, if the host blog allows links in the comments. Make sure to tick the "follow up" alerts box so that you will know when someone else has replied to your comment, and you can keep the conversation going.

RISK FACTOR: MEDIUM TO HIGH

#16 COMMENT REGULARLY ON OTHER BLOGS

BLOGGER STORY

"Commenting on other blogs has been incredibly important to my growth as a blogger, and to the growth of my business.

"It's a way of getting to know other people, it builds community, and it can be a doorway to guest blogging. As I look through the comments on my blog posts, I very often check out those who are commenting. I not only visit their blogs, but sometimes I'll comment if I have something to say. I know that quite a few of the folks who visit and comment on my blog first discovered me in the comment section of other blogs."

KEN MUELLER, INKLINGMEDIA.NET

" EXPERT COMMENT

"Many comments are usually quickly composed affairs, resulting from the natural impulse to 'have your say,' and these do have their time and place. But if you have an ulterior motive of creating awareness about you and what you do, spreading knowledge to benefit others, helping others out of kindness, forming new blogging relationships, or even gaining more traffic back to your blog, the practice of writing great comments is more likely to result in a positive and responsible outcome."

ALICE ELLIOTT, WWW.FAIRYBLOGMOTHER.CO.UK

"Commenting can be a doorway to guest blogging."

KEN MUELLER

#17 KEEP THE LOOK CLEAN & UNCLUTTERED

A BLOG SHOULD BE CLEAR AND EASY TO READ, FREE FROM TOO MANY WIDGETS, ADVERTISEMENTS, AND OTHER DISTRACTIONS THAT MAKE IT HARD TO FIND THE GOOD CONTENT. CLUTTER IS OFF-PUTTING FOR VISITORS WHO DON'T HAVE TIME TO WADE THROUGH IT ALL.

Where it comes from:

The word "clean," when used in a design sense, is loaded with connotations. Not clean? Must be dirty then! Your blog is your online home, and when you open your doors you want it to be fresh and welcoming to visitors. But there's a difference between not having vacuumed in a year and choosing to cover your walls with pictures and your shelves with trinkets. Clutter doesn't necessary make it unhygienic; it just may not be to everyone's taste. The twentieth-century modernists began the war against excessive ornamentation in design and architecture, and on the web it's no different: minimal and subtle still passes as smart and sophisticated; busy and in-your-face does not. Web usability experts say it's more than a matter of taste—because everyone is so time-poor, and because when we go online it's usually to do something or find something; too much clutter can get in the way of good, clear communication.

WHEN TO BREAK THE RULE

This is a tricky one. Your blog is your property, and how it looks is entirely up to you. In the same way that not everyone has a clutter-free home, it should ultimately be down to what pleases you. Perhaps animated gifs make you smile and you want to share that with others who feel the same way. Maybe the subject matter of your blog lends itself to busy, excitable design features. Perhaps your chosen colors or logo are not subtle, but there's a valid reason. Your blog needs to be consistent with other aspects of how you present yourself in business, or your personality. Perhaps you're just a sucker for fun widgets, jazzy icons, and loads of STUFF on your blog.

If you've made a deliberate decision to break the clean-and-minimal rule, then that's OK—as long as you understand the risks. Have you considered what the busy look says about you, and are you happy with that? How important is it to you that some visitors will be put off from reading your blog, or have trouble finding the actual content? Are you interested in what the experts say is "good" or "poor" blog design, or can they all go take a running jump? If you think your blog might be breaking this rule, and you'd like to do something about it, it may just be a case of a few small tweaks. Rein back a little on the sidebar widgets or simplify the color scheme, for example. Try a new theme or template. All is not lost.

RISK FACTOR: HIGH

#17 KEEP THE LOOK CLEAN & UNCLUTTERED

EXPERT COMMENT

"One of the biggest things a blogger should remember about design is white space, more white space, and a little more white space. Increasing spacing in between products or items on the page makes each stand out and really helps them not get lost in the crowd. You can ALWAYS tell a graphic designer's blog—it's visually SO clean because they know a thing or two about white space. A good tip from a blogging perspective is to remember that you always want readers to stay on your blog as long as possible, so don't cram your roundup into a graphic that can be seen in one shot. Making something a little longer in size (a.k.a. increasing the white space!), ensures people keep on scrollin', baby."

ERIN HIEMSTRA, WWW.APARTMENT34.COM

"You can always tell a graphic designer's blog because they know a thing or two about white space."

ERIN HIEMSTRA

EXPERT COMMENT

"Minimal design has been glorified from each corner of the web. So much so that young designers consider clean style/minimal design to be the only ultimate approach. But the world is bigger than that—in a lot of cases cluttered/magazine-style designs can also look great—take a look at the online presences of *Wired*, *Cosmopolitan*, or the BBC, for starters. Online magazines and news agency websites are often what you'd call 'cluttered', but they work. When you need to deliver tons of information from the home page to your visitors, there is no place for a minimal solution because you must use every single pixel wisely and prudently."

EDWARD KORCHEG, WWW.TEMPLATEMONSTER.COM

#18 DO NOT STEAL

IF YOU WANT TO POST SOMEONE ELSE'S WORDS, PHOTOS, OR OTHER CONTENT ON YOUR BLOG, YOU SHOULD ASK PERMISSION FIRST, AND GIVE PROPER ATTRIBUTION. PERIOD.

Where it comes from:

It's hard to argue with the moral imperative of the eighth commandment. Unfortunately, the ease and speed with which material may be copied and spread on the internet, combined with a certain amount of ignorance, has created a perfect storm surrounding the issue of intellectual property. There are also various legal gray areas due to the cross-border nature of the web and notions such as fair usage. And then there's the problem of how difficult it can sometimes be to contact or even to identify copyright owners.

Social sharing has become second nature, and there's no way that (for example) every photo shared on Facebook comes with a photographer credit. It's just too easy to forget the differences between sharing, borrowing, and stealing, so we need reminding.

WHEN TO BREAK THE RULE

It's not so much a question of breaking this rule, but breaking
it down. Some people would argue there are degrees of stealing;
for others it is clearly black and white.

Let's say for example that you are inspired by an article and want
to share it on your blog. So you write your own blog post and
include short extracts from the original article to illustrate or back
up what you want to say. If the extracts are just a few lines, the
law might regard that as OK, as long as you credit your source.
But if it's half the original article, with no credit, that might be
seen as a breach of copyright. (Notice I'm saying *might*—laws
vary and this is for illustrative purposes; it is not legal advice.)
Then again, some blog platforms encourage reblogging—where
an entire blog post is reposted to your own blog. The original
blogger may get an alert when this happens, but their permission
is implicit in the terms of the blogging platform they are using.
So if you "reblog" someone's post, you're not obliged to ask
permission from the original author.

If you simply copy and paste an article and pass it off as your
own, most people would agree that is stealing. But so is posting
a photo without permission from the copyright holder and
without the proper credits. Just because an image or a poem
or a song has been posted umpteen times across the web, don't
assume it's free to use on your blog. Even if your investigations
convince you that it is, at the very least you should state where
you found it and include a link to that source.

RISK FACTOR: HIGH

#18 DO NOT STEAL

EXPERT COMMENT

"Some of the best blog posts piggyback off of someone else's work. It's okay to steal ideas as long as you don't steal the actual work. Here are some examples:

1) Scan other blog post headlines until something jumps out at you (don't click through). Then, rewrite the headline, maybe using a related (not identical) keyword. Write your blog post for that new headline.
2) Borrow a list item. Take one list item from a great blog post and expound on that on your own blog.
3) Quote from a popular blog. Find a paragraph or a sentence in a blog post that strikes you as interesting, and quote it, adding your own commentary. Always link back to the original post."

CAROLINE MELBERG, WWW.SMALLBUSINESSMAVERICKS.COM

"If you 'closely imitate' the work of another, changing a few words, it's still plagiarism."

VAHNI LEVITT

BLOGGER STORY

"We all know verbatim copying without attribution is illegal and unacceptable, and that blog scrapers (people who copy content, often using software to scan hundreds of blogs) are clearly committing copyright infringement. But plagiarism doesn't pertain only to verbatim regurgitation of another's writing. If you 'closely imitate' the work of another, changing a few words here and there, you're still guilty of plagiarism.

"This is exactly what happened to two fellow bloggers and me when our content was stolen by another blogger and passed off as her own. And you know what was funny? The very blogger who lifted our content offered a pretty good explanation of it in a post she dedicated to preaching about plagiarism.

"We fought back and won—and although we did successfully retrieve our content, it's extremely frustrating knowing she continues to represent herself as an 'honest' writer who would never, ever plagiarize."

VAHNI LEVITT, WWW.GRITANDGLAMOUR.COM

#19 OPTIMIZE EVERY POST WITH KEYWORDS

YOU SHOULD ALWAYS INCLUDE RELEVANT KEYWORDS IN YOUR BLOG POSTS, OTHERWISE THEY MAY NOT GET FOUND OR READ. USE WHITE HAT TECHNIQUES (ETHICAL SEO TECHNIQUES AIMED AT THE HUMAN AUDIENCE AND NOT THE SEARCH ENGINE) ONLY. YOU SHOULD ALSO DO KEYWORD RESEARCH SO YOU CAN PLACE QUALITY KEYWORDS AND PHRASES INTO YOUR POSTS THAT WILL GET THE ATTENTION OF THE SEARCH ENGINES, AND LET THEM KNOW WHAT YOUR POST IS ABOUT. THINK ABOUT WHAT SOMEONE WOULD TYPE INTO GOOGLE IF THEY WERE LOOKING FOR THE INFORMATION PROVIDED IN YOUR POST, AND TRY TO SLIP THOSE WORDS OR PHRASES INTO YOUR ARTICLE A FEW TIMES EACH.

Where it comes from:
It's easy to be invisible on the web, and search engines used to be the only way for your web content to be found. After website design, search engine optimization (SEO) was probably the biggest internet industry in the early days of the web.

One of the reasons why a web page appears in search results is because the word or phrase being searched for appears on that page. So all you need to do is figure out what words people are searching for, and include them in your page copy and in various places throughout the source code. Simple! Except it's not that simple. It's actually the science of search engine optimization, or SEO, and millions of minds are employed in trying to think like a search engine robot in order to get web page A above web page B in the search results.

WHEN TO BREAK THE RULE

They're still important, but search engines are no longer the only route to being found. Visitors are just as likely to arrive at your blog via links shared on social networks or other blogs. Nevertheless, it's a good idea to research your keywords, because their application goes beyond just being found on Google. You can spend a lot of time on this, but you don't have to. What words or phrases are your potential readers searching for? Ask friends. Look at your blog stats. Check out the successful blogs in your niche. Do some searches and see what blogs come up. Think about the topics you talk about most on your blog. Make a list. Some you might make Categories. When you write a blog post, decide on no more than two keywords/phrases relevant to that post. Try to use them in the headline and a couple of times in the first paragraph. Use them to tag images and the blog post itself. If you have an SEO plug-in such as Yoast, include your keywords in the metadata. Use them in social updates that refer to the blog post.

It's easy to get bogged down by SEO. If you're a large corporate institution or an online business, such as a price comparison site, SEO will be mission-critical and you will find the budget for it—which can be vast. SEO is about much more than keywords—search engines also look for good quality inbound links, frequency and recency of posting, authority, and more. For the majority of blogs, a few well-researched keywords inserted in the relevant places will make a big difference. But don't beat yourself up if you don't do it for every post.

RISK FACTOR: LOW TO MEDIUM

#19 OPTIMIZE EVERY POST WITH KEYWORDS

EXPERT COMMENT

"Most bloggers don't blog full-time, at least not at the beginning, so they don't have thousands of dollars to spend. Of all the free traffic-generation methods, utilizing keywords on your blog is the first and most obvious. But my advice would be to shift your focus away from short-tail, highly competitive keywords and instead find some low-hanging fruit in the form of longer, more specific search queries. When I tried this on one of my own blogs last year, I found search traffic increased by over 450%—not bad. What's more, visitors were staying on the site because the content was directly relevant to the query they were searching for."

MATTHEW BARBY, WWW.MATTHEWBARBY.COM

"Shift your focus away from highly competitive keywords and toward long-tail, more specific search terms."

MATTHEW BARBY

BLOGGER STORY

"Personal stylist service iStylista.com have never advertised themselves—instead they have produced excellent online PR from their blogs and their networking skills around the blogosphere. Co-founder Hayden Allen-Vercoe says their success was bolstered by starting to write a keyword rich blog that pushed up their rankings and doubled their sales:

"'We do keyword research for every article we post. We look at what the competition is doing, and we use Wordtracker (a keyword research tool) to death. We search for things like 'maxi dress' and I'll get all these keywords and then write the article around the keywords.'

"Although this is a relatively good technique, Allen-Vercoe warned against writing articles that look staged. Your blog entry needs to have flow and make sense to the reader without feeling labored by your inclusion of keywords."

RACHELLE MONEY, WWW.WORDTRACKER.COM

#20 IT'S ALL ABOUT THE NUMBERS

NUMBERS MATTER. IF YOU'RE NOT MEASURING AND ASSESSING YOUR BLOG STATS, THEN YOU CAN'T POSSIBLY KNOW IF YOUR BLOG IS SUCCESSFUL OR IF YOU'RE JUST WASTING YOUR TIME.

Where it comes from:

The business world loves quantitative data. We can always have an idea about what's working and what isn't, but you can't argue with hard data. It's the arbiter of budgetary spend. If you can't show the positive impact of your activity on the bottom line, questions are asked: Why are we doing this? Business bloggers can't help but be interested in the stats, because a business blog either has to make money directly or facilitate the making of money. It has to earn its way. Adding further fuel to this particular fire is the fact that internet activity is so wonderfully measurable. Everything that can be counted will be counted.

WHEN TO BREAK THE RULE

The data-centric view of blogging says that it doesn't matter if you produce the most original, mind-blowing content, or if the design is cutting edge, or if your photographs are more beautiful than anyone else's, or any other qualitative measure you choose to value. These things only matter if they can be shown to be contributing to the positive statistics—for example, increasing visitors, subscribers, sign-ups, and sales.

Not every blogger is in it to make a profit: hobbyists, passionate enthusiasts, creative people—they may have very different goals and different notions of what success looks like. But also, not every blog is at the stage where there is enough data to support every decision. Your long-term goal may be to monetize your blog, but your short- to medium-terms goals need to be at least as focused on qualitative factors. There is so much great content on the web already, so many eye-catching blogs. There needs to be a compelling reason for people to subscribe to yours, and it takes time and effort to build an audience. The cost of this effort is likely to be disproportionate to the payback for some time. And let's not forget that numbers can also be misleading. It's crucial to measure the relevant things and not pay undue attention to everything else. For example, rather than just checking how many page views your blog is getting, look instead at which of your blog posts are receiving the most attention over time. This can be quite an eye-opener and give you valuable insights into what people enjoy reading about, so (should you wish) you can produce more of the same.

RISK FACTOR: MEDIUM TO HIGH

#20 IT'S ALL ABOUT THE NUMBERS

" EXPERT COMMENT

"It was Peter Druker, an American management consultant who stated 'if you can't measure it, you can't manage it,' and this is true whether you are a multinational business with a strategic plan or a hobbyist blogger who wants to know whether anyone is reading your blog.

"There has been a shift in recent years of what metrics are important to people. It used to be about analyzing traffic to websites and the number of followers you had, but with people realizing it is now as much about Return on Engagement as it is Return on Investment, this is all shifting. Site visits and follower counts mean nothing without engagement in today's digital marketing world.

"Therefore, knowing what you want to achieve and putting metrics in place to monitor is a fundamental prerequisite to any website, campaign, or strategy."

JAMES DEARSLEY, WWW.THEDIGITALMARKETINGBUREAU.COM

BLOGGER STORY

"Here's the truth: Most bloggers are being controlled. Their articles, content, styles, and brands are being dictated by the 'rules' of traditional blogging. Some rules are necessary, such as 'Don't spam other blogs.' Those are important. But one I refuse to follow is 'the goal is page views.' More and more bloggers realize that building community and getting the right people on your email list is more important than page views. I would rather get 500 responsive email subscribers than 10,000 page views and no one signing up any day. Wouldn't you?"

HECTOR CUEVAS, WWW.INBOUNDPRO.NET

"Site visits and follower counts mean nothing without engagement in today's digital marketing world."

JAMES DEARSLEY

#21 DEVELOP BLOGGING BUDDIES

**OTHER BLOGGERS ARE YOUR FRIENDS, NOT YOUR ENEMIES.
A SUPPORTIVE NETWORK OF BLOGGING BUDDIES WILL DO WONDERS
FOR YOUR REPUTATION AND YOUR BLOG. PUT YOUR ENERGY INTO
THIS RATHER THAN TRYING TO KEEP DOWN THE COMPETITION.**

Where it comes from:
At the beginning of the twentieth century, there weren't many
motor cars on the roads. If you were a motorist and you passed
a broken-down car, you would stop to help, which usually meant
both of you getting under the hood trying to figure out the
problem. The internet used to be like that: fewer people, and
mostly pioneer-spirited enthusiasts coping with unreliable
technology. In a matter of months you were an "old hand,"
and the old hands were generous, shared what they knew,
and welcomed bewildered newbies. There was a saying that
"information wants to be free." Things may be different now,
but scratch the surface and there
is generosity and goodwill
almost everywhere you
look, particularly in the
blogging world. It's not
all altruistic: having
a team of blogging
buddies will help
bring you more
exposure, new readers,
added authority, and
amazing opportunities.

WHEN TO BREAK THE RULE

One of the appeals of blogging is the freedom of expression it gives people. Not everybody blogs within a supportive niche, or wants to have blogging buddies. Some bloggers thrive on controversy. Others have a strong sense of what they want to say and how they want to say it, and won't compromise on that, even if it risks causing offence. Choose your blogging buddies wisely. If you're blogging on behalf of your business, you're unlikely to offer a competitor the facility of guest posting, but you might have a good enough relationship to suggest a collaboration of some kind. If you are open to cooperating with other bloggers, there are countless ways to develop good relationships with them, and it almost always pays off. Take the initiative by linking generously, and if you ask for a favor, make sure you offer something in return. Blogging can be a hard and lonely business.

Don't forget that playing nice also means not breaching other people's copyright and not libeling people. A blogger is also a publisher, and there are laws in your country that govern what you can and can't publish.

RISK FACTOR: LOW

#21 DEVELOP BLOGGING BUDDIES

EXPERT COMMENT

"Finding that special blogging buddy (or buddies) isn't anything you can place on Craig's List. There are a number of things to bear in mind. For example, offer assistance wherever needed and whenever possible. Most people would agree that the adage 'what goes around comes around' is mostly on the money. Even more so in Blogopolis. Everyone playing the game is new, even those who have been in it since before the beginning. Lending a hand when you find yourself in a position to do so is not only kind, but it will most likely be remembered later. However, NEVER be overly eager or desperate! As in life, this tactic will not help in the search for a blogging partner. It is important to remain cool and collected. The right decision is rarely made in desperation."

SEAN PLATT, SEANMPLATT.COM

"Finding that special blogging buddy (or buddies) isn't anything you can place on Craig's List."

SEAN PLATT

BLOGGER STORY

"In 2011, I got super serious about my writing career and thought I had to have an online presence, so I got back into blogging. I posted. I committed to doing it once a week, then once a week flew by, and I committed to once every two weeks. I allowed my fiction writing to eat up all of my free time. Years passed. No one cared if I posted anyway, there was no accountability.

"Now, I've finished a few books and short stories. I'm submitting to publishers. But again I needed to get out of my writer's hidey hole; I needed to connect.

"I hit upon my answer when I discovered group blogging. Some of the pressure released. If I don't have much to say, then I call on my blog mates to help. And if I don't post, there are people who depend on me, which raises the stakes of not performing. And in those long, lonely days when I believe no one reads, I know that at least my blog mates will be checking."

PAMELA STEWART, WWW.SMASHEDPICKETFENCES.COM

#22 GUEST POSTING HELPS WITH SEO

WRITING GUEST POSTS ON HIGHLY TRAFFICKED BLOGS IS A GOOD WAY OF INCREASING THE VISIBILITY OF YOUR OWN BLOG AND GETTING HIGHER RANKINGS IN SEARCH RESULTS.

Where it comes from:
Link building used to be a standard tactic for search-engine optimizers. The way it worked was that the more inbound links you could get to your website the better, because the search-engine robots would follow those links to your site and award you points for authority (if all those sites are linking to yours, it must have something, right?). In the early 2000s, this was a big part of SEO—finding relevant web directories and listings sites where you could put a link and a description back to your own. But, as with many internet early practices, it got abused and the search engines changed the rules. Actually they keep changing them, since "black hat" SEO (finding ways to game or scam the search engines) has become a huge industry.

Genuine inbound links from relevant, high-traffic sites will still confer authority on your blog. As will having a big name blogger agree to write a guest post on your humble blog. But industrial-scale guest posting on low-quality sites purely for the purpose of gaining inbound links is no longer viable. Google has made it clear that the free "link juice" has run out, and that guest posting purely for SEO won't work. In any case, the majority of links from other blogs to yours will be "nofollow"—meaning that search robots are instructed to disregard them.

#22

WHEN TO BREAK THE RULE

Is guest posting for SEO really dead? Industry experts are still
arguing about this. The evidence is that links from relevant,
high-quality blogs can still bring SEO benefits. But that
shouldn't be your number one reason to write (or accept) guest
blog posts. The real benefits are from a branding or reputation
point of view. A guest blog post on an appropriate website or
blog will bring you to the attention of a whole new audience.
You don't have to shoot for Lifehacker or nytimes.com—yes
they have big audiences, but an appearance on an authoritative,
relevant site in your niche may do you just as much good. To be
read by a highly targeted, probably highly engaged, audience will
increase your blog's reach, authority, and reputation. So guest
posting isn't dead, it's just less important for SEO.

RISK FACTOR: MEDIUM

#22 GUEST POSTING HELPS WITH SEO

EXPERT COMMENT

"Guest blogging is still a match made in heaven in term of SEO as long as the website where your guest post is shared is of quality and the links being included in your content are of quality as well. Inbound links from quality sources will help continue to associate your website with the correct keywords, as well as help grow your authority once these links are shared across social media. Links to your guest blog posts on social media play a huge factor in what websites are ranked for what keyword phrases in the search engines. Growing your audience with guest blogging will impact your SEO through increased social media growth, stronger industry visibility, more networking opportunities, and growing brand recognition."

BRIAN HONIGMAN, WWW.BRIANHONIGMAN.COM

"It may be on Google's radar, but I wouldn't close the coffin lid on guest blogging just yet."

ELISA GABBERT

" EXPERT COMMENT

"It may be on Google's radar, but I wouldn't close the coffin lid on guest blogging just yet. If an SEO tactic works, then it will get more and more spammy with time; there is no spam-proof SEO technique. Every technique has to adapt over time with the competitive landscape and the algorithm. Likewise, marketers always need to focus on long-view quality over short-term effectiveness, regardless of the technique. But just because spammers start doing something doesn't mean you have to stop.

"In fact, I might argue that few SEO techniques get 'more and more spammy' by proportion. In other words, they're not going from 10% spammy to 50% spammy. You just see more spam because there's more of everything— more good guest posts, but more crap and spam too. Eventually there's so much of everything, good and bad, that it becomes very difficult for Google to sort through it all. They get frustrated and try to tell us, the content creators, to police ourselves so they don't have to. There's no foolproof way for Google to determine the motives of any given author, whether they wrote and published something for links, exposure, money, or pure altruism."

ELISA GABBERT, WWW.WORDSTREAM.COM

#23 ENGAGE YOUR AUDIENCE

BLOGGERS SHOULD DO ALL THEY CAN TO INVOLVE READERS, BECAUSE WHEN READERS ARE ENGAGED THEY ARE MORE LIKELY TO KEEP READING, COMING BACK, AND SHARING YOUR BLOG CONTENT WITH THEIR NETWORKS.

Where it comes from:
Twenty-first-century marketers love buzzwords like "engagement." The engaged audience has become a kind of holy grail for businesses trying to exploit social media for promotional purposes. For many people this is reason enough to hate the term.

If you can get beyond the hype, the idea is a pretty basic one. When we are interested in something, we pay attention. If we take it a step further and get involved in some way, and are rewarded for it, we're likely to do it again—and so on. Once you start thinking about it, you might come to the conclusion that just about everything we do in life is based on this incentive-reward reinforcement loop. But let's stick to blogging for now. Experience has shown that if a blogger encourages and then rewards reader involvement (for example, by acknowledging great comments, thanking people for subscribing, creating exclusive offers or access to products, inviting readers to guest post, or in myriad other creative ways), it leads to higher reader numbers, more shares, more social kudos, and all the associated opportunities these things bring. In short, keeping your audience engaged leads to a more successful blog.

WHEN TO BREAK THE RULE

This is a fine rule, but there a many degrees of engagement, and not all bloggers have the same goals. It's also important to realize that readers may be engaged on any number of levels. It's not just about how many people respond to a poll.

Most blogs start out small. For a while you may wonder if you're talking to thin air, so the joy of receiving your first comment or subscriber is indescribable. Even though the initial excitement wears off, you get into the habit of thanking people for their comments and trying to encourage more. You learn the importance of engaging readers so you try holding the odd poll, or competition. Then one day you realize you're spending all your time responding to comments, replying to emails, and all the rest—rather than creating blog posts.

For many, this is all part of the fun of blogging, but for others it becomes a distraction and a timesuck. At this stage, many bloggers lose enthusiasm or even give up. Others keep at it and find a way of managing—by bringing in help, by using automation where possible, by telling enquirers not to always expect a reply, and so on. There is a risk: the reader may feel distanced, or the blog might seem less personal. But time and again, bloggers find the emails and comments keep coming, and people keep subscribing and sharing. So they're doing something right—they're producing great blog posts, sharing their passion in original ways, and creating a valuable blog that engages readers.

RISK FACTOR: MEDIUM TO HIGH

ENGAGE YOUR AUDIENCE

EXPERT COMMENT

"One sure-fire way to skyrocket your reader engagement is to write the kind of content people crave.

"Content that inspires: Blog posts that remind people the life is short, that every human is important, to believe in bigger things, and that dreams do come true.

"Content that connects with emotions: Things that make your readers cry, laugh, or shock them in amazement.

"Content that tells stories: That takes people on a journey, reveals secrets, and teaches them to never give up. Stories where the underdog wins.

"Content that teaches: Content that gives your audience action steps and life lessons, challenges their thinking, and tells them what to do next. Gives them very practical, hands-on tips and makes them smarter."

MARYA JAN, WWW.GETRESPONSE.COM

EXPERT COMMENT

"The goal of blogging is not to prove how smart you are. It's not to stand on a soapbox and proffer your opinion of the world. No one wants to hear that. Instead, the goal of blogging is to make a genuine connection with your reader, pure and simple. That connection should lead to a lasting and deeper relationship between reader and blogger. Like any relationship, you don't want to talk TO your audience, you want to talk WITH them. Ask the reader's opinion. Elicit their feedback. Solve their problems. Ask for their vote. Pose questions. Make it about THEM and the value you can bring to their lives, and they'll love you for it. That is engagement."

NORM SCHRIEVER, WWW.NORMSCHRIEVER.COM

"Like any relationship, you don't want to talk TO your readers, you want to talk WITH them."

NORM SCHRIEVER

#24 ANYONE CAN MAKE MONEY FROM BLOGGING

ANYONE CAN MAKE MONEY FROM BLOGGING. YOU JUST HAVE TO WORK VERY HARD, DO YOUR RESEARCH, AND FOLLOW THE BEST ADVICE AVAILABLE.

Where it comes from:
There's something about the pioneering landscape of the web that fills people with optimism. Just as any American citizen can potentially grow up to be the President, so too can anyone make their fortune on the internet. There are plenty of examples, some high profile, others less so, of bloggers who gave up the day job and are now blogging, speaking, or consulting for a living. Many (but not all) were early movers—they seized the opportunity when the blogosphere was still relatively small and there were fortunes to be made.

WHEN TO BREAK THE RULE

People are certainly making money from blogging, both directly and indirectly. Compare success stories and you will find common denominators: the willingness to work very hard and to suffer privations, often for no money or little payback for years; a large amount of self-belief and determination; the ability to convert luck and opportunity to their advantage. And that's really just for starters. On the other hand, many bloggers start off wanting to make blogging pay but find they derive enough satisfaction from other aspects of blogging. Making money becomes less of a priority.

The evidence suggests that *some* people can make *some* money from blogging, and a *very small percentage* of people make *a lot* of money from it. In other words, very few people get rich from it. On his blog, ProBlogger (www.problogger.com), Darren Rowse disclosed exactly which revenue streams worked for him proportionally to others: by far the biggest earner for him was Google AdSense small display ads (250 × 300 pixels), followed by affiliate programs, e-book sales, continuity programs, and private ad sales or sponsorships, amongst other things.

There's a difference between making money directly from a blog, and indirectly because of a blog. For example, consulting work, speaking engagements, writing jobs, and business partnerships might all come the way of a successful blogger. Rather than thinking of blogging as a way to get rich, it might be more realistic to focus on the enhanced opportunities it may bring.

RISK FACTOR: MEDIUM

#24 ANYONE CAN MAKE MONEY FROM BLOGGING

BLOGGER STORY

"I met Fran Kerr of HighOnHealth.org back in 2007 and realized she had the talent to go after the blogging business model. Fran really experienced a rollercoaster of emotions—almost giving up completely at one stage—before finally tasting success. The challenge in the end came down to mind-set more than anything else—and having a coach and mentor really made a difference.

"Fran now has one of the most popular alternative health- and skincare blogs in the world. She writes articles for her blog, produces videos that she shares on her YouTube channel and her blog, has a subscriber base of over 15,000 people, sells e-books, has an e-commerce store where she sells physical products, has a membership site, and does affiliate marketing.

"Fran is a hard worker who followed my systems and advice sometimes, while at other times she did things her own way. Today, the monthly income from Fran's blog-based business is anywhere from $4,000 to $12,000 a month."

YARO STARAK, WWW.ENTREPRENEURS-JOURNEY.COM

BLOGGER STORY

"I was over the moon when I was first invited to join an advertising program. At the end of 40 days of dancing, flashing ads taking up prime real estate on my blog, I'd made a grand total of $5.85. And I wouldn't see a dime until I reached $100. That was the end of that.

"There are a handful of bloggers who make a lot of money blogging. I don't know any of them personally, but they must exist. And then there are a lot of bloggers who make some money experimenting with different strategies and revenue streams. Do what works for you and your readers."

AIMEE WHETSTINE, EVERYDAYEPISTLE.COM

"The challenge in the end comes down to mind-set more than anything else."

YARO STARAK

#25 BUILD AN EMAIL LIST

BLOGGERS NEED TO BUILD AN EMAIL LIST IN ORDER TO CAPTURE THE NAMES AND ADDRESSES OF PEOPLE INTERESTED IN THEIR BLOG. THE BLOGGER CAN THEN REACH OUT TO THEM DIRECTLY WITH NEWS OR OFFERS.

Where it comes from:

Email? Haven't we been told for years that email is dead, that Gen Y never use it, that spam has destroyed any usefulness it once had? Guess what—email is still hanging in there. In fact, it's as relevant as ever. There was a time when the humble email newsletter took a battering, when spam seemed to be engulfing the internet and turning people off the idea of signing up for anything. The spam may have got spammier, but spam filters are smarter, email service providers are more compliant, and we've all become a lot more expert at spotting and avoiding the scams. The importance of email to bloggers is this: when blog subscribers opt to read your blog, they're not giving you permission to contact them directly other than via your blog updates. Although it's possible to see who your followers are, harvesting their email addresses isn't straightforward, and if you were to start emailing them on that basis you would lose followers fast. However, encouraging people to sign up to an email list is a legitimate way of identifying your pre-qualified audience (that is, people already interested in what you have to say, or what you're selling) and, crucially, sending them messages. If you're blogging for business reasons—to build relationships with prospects and customers, or simply to sell—start building an email list.

WHEN TO BREAK THE RULE

Not every blogger is selling something, and not everyone wants the added burden of an email newsletter. Adding an email sign-up box to your blog is quick and easy to do, especially if you use one of the free, popular email marketing services that integrate with blogging software, such as MailChimp. But it's also a responsibility. It means you have to email something out. Many experts say that it's never too soon to start collecting email addresses. However, if people sign up for an email list and don't hear from you for ages, chances are when they do finally receive something they'll have forgotten they subscribed in the first place and either unsubscribe or mark it as spam. If you're blogging for fun and short of time, the idea of creating and sending email updates as well as keeping your blog going might not fill you with enthusiasm. In which case, don't worry about the email list. You can start building it when you have something to say.

RISK FACTOR: MEDIUM TO HIGH

#25 BUILD AN EMAIL LIST

BLOGGER STORY

"I was talking to my publisher the other day about marketing strategies for my next book, and do you know the first question they asked? 'How big is your email list?' Not: 'How many RSS subscribers do you have?' or: 'How many hits does your blog get?'

"Nope. None of that. Just email—the most important tool you need to get your message heard. Musicians use it to get word out about their next tour. Writers use it to announce an upcoming book. Retailers use it to share special deals and drive sales. It's all about the list. Email isn't dead—every day, people check their inboxes (often multiple times per day).

"As a writer, I get more mileage out of my newsletter than any other platform I have—including my blog. When I send an email to my list, I often get hundreds of replies—far more engagement than many of my blog posts get. If I send a link to my email list, people click it. If I ask a question, people answer. If I talk about my new book, people buy. Email is still the most powerful way to communicate online."

JEFF GOINS, GOINSWRITER.COM

EXPERT COMMENT

"Email marketing and a blog serve different purposes, and a smart content-marketing program will usually include both.

"A blog serves to attract the attention of new prospects, as well as building your reputation in your topic. A blog is a place to be publicly seen—to show your expertise and your passion for your subject. They're ideal for meeting new people, and giving those people an easy way to find out more about you and what you do.

"An email newsletter is about deepening the relationship. Without getting the attention of potential customers, you have no marketing program. But if you never do anything with that attention, you have no business. They work together."

SONIA SIMONE, WWW.COPYBLOGGER.COM

"Email is still the most powerful way to communicate online."

JEFF GOINS

#26 MAKE YOUR CONTENT SHAREABLE

IF YOU WANT YOUR BLOG TO BE SEEN AND READ AND IF YOU WANT NEW READERS, THEN YOU SHOULD MAKE IT EASY, NOT DIFFICULT, FOR PEOPLE TO SHARE ITS CONTENT IN WHICHEVER WAY THEY WISH.

Where it comes from:

Before the growth of social networks, there was little attention paid to the sharing of content. Articles, photos, video—whatever was on your website (or blog, in blogging's early days) stayed where it was. There were email newsletters with "forward to a friend" links. When people started sharing content it was on social bookmarking sites, such as StumbleUpon and Delicious, with technology, news, and business content leading the way. Since the birth of Facebook and Twitter, and the upsurge in mobile usage and apps, such as Instagram, sharing is now mainstream. Everyone wants to be sharing—publicly, privately, to certain groups of particular contacts and not others—and doing so is expected to be easy and seamless. Bloggers have access to endless social-sharing apps, widgets, and icons. Blog visitors want to be able to share something they like, rate and comment on it, all in an instant and on whatever device they are using.

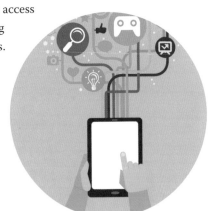

WHEN TO BREAK THE RULE

This is a pretty good rule, and it's hard to imagine a good reason to break it. If you have objections from an aesthetic point of view (not wanting prominent share icons or buttons to spoil the cool look of your blog), then you can always get a designer to create something bespoke. Research has shown that blogs with share buttons get mentioned seven times as much as those without, so it's a no-brainer. It's also worth checking your stats once in a while to see which platforms your readers are sharing on. If nobody is sharing your articles on Digg or Google+, you could delete that option. More importantly, you can find out where your content is being shared the most, and feature that place more prominently, even start using it yourself more. If your blog has a following on Facebook, perhaps you could make more of that. Of course, share buttons are only one way of making content easy for people to share, as Pamela Vaughan from HubSpot reminds us over the page...

RISK FACTOR: MEDIUM TO HIGH

#26 MAKE YOUR CONTENT SHAREABLE

💬 EXPERT COMMENT

"There are a number of ways to make sharing simple, for example:

1. Keep your article titles brief. Certain social media sites—like Twitter—limit the number of characters that can be used in a post or update. When people share an article, they often like to include some of their own commentary with it. Keep in mind that the post will also need to leave room for a shortened URL to the content itself. Don't take up that precious social media real estate with a long title.

2. Add enticing meta descriptions. When you share a post on sites like Facebook, LinkedIn, and Google+, they automatically pull in a description of the post. Most sites generate this description from the URL's meta description. Be sure each blog post, web page, and landing page you create includes an enticing meta description to motivate social media users to check out your content.

3. Make sure your content is high in quality...Focus most of your energy on creating high-quality content, and usually, the shares will follow."

PAMELA VAUGHAN, WWW.HUBSPOT.COM

> ## 🗨 EXPERT COMMENT

"You don't have to use all the social networks and build a following of 100,000 people before you start seeing the benefits of social sharing. The more practical, useful, and valuable your content is, the more people will click the share button and spread your message with their network. But it's your job to build those relationships on the social networks first. Be social and people will help you spread the word."

HECTOR CUEVAS, WWW.INBOUNDPRO.NET

"Focus most of your energy on creating high-quality content, and the shares will follow."

PAMELA VAUGHAN

#27 EASE UP ON THE HARD SELL

CONSTANTLY BLASTING OUT SALES MESSAGES ON YOUR BLOG OR USING SPAMMY SALES TACTICS IS COUNTERPRODUCTIVE, AS IT WILL PUT PEOPLE OFF.

Where it comes from:
There has always been a tension between sales and marketing. Sales people complain that marketers spend all the money on fluffy stuff like advertising, while it's sales people who actually close deals and earn money. Marketers complain that since their work is less quantifiable, they get less of the glory while salesfolk get all the bonuses. The truth is, if you don't invest in marketing, you have to work harder at selling, and vice versa. This could mean sending out millions of unsolicited email messages in the knowledge that all you need is a conversion rate of a fraction of a percent to make it worthwhile. Or it could mean constantly reminding your followers or sign-ups of reasons to buy. But being sold to twenty-four seven is no joke.

If you can find a way to temper the sales messages with less direct ways of demonstrating value, and keep communications targeted and personal (so people don't feel they're being broadcast to), then you'll have more long-term success.

WHEN TO BREAK THE RULE

Is telling people about what you're selling (on your blog, by email, or on social networks) really spammy, or an acceptable way to make people aware of it—helpful even?

The hard sell is popular on the web because the numbers stack up. The web is overflowing with case studies proving this point. So it's down to your goals as a blogger. If you're interested in making money in the shortest possible time, learn all the hard-sell tactics and develop a thick skin. If you're more in the business of building relationships and reputation in order to gain referrals, build a network of friends/prospects, and maybe monetize your power base in the future, then ease up on the hard sell. (The really clever people blend both these strategies.)

A common piece of advice is to look at what the biggest and most successful bloggers are doing and emulate it. The trouble is, it's not always obvious how the high-visibility bloggers got to where they did. Nor is it obvious how this apparently successful tactic fits with everything else they do, such as producing high-quality, useful content for free: webinars, Twitter chats, white papers, in-depth resources, giveaways...and all of it in addition to well-researched and informative blog posts. The more high-value, useful stuff you're prepared to give away, the more forgiving people will be of hard-sell techniques and self promotion, and you can afford to play loose with this rule.

RISK FACTOR: MEDIUM TO HIGH

#27 EASE UP ON THE HARD SELL

"Quite a few of the top bloggers don't sell anything on their blog. That's right—no banner ads, no pitches on the bottom of posts, no pages full of affiliate products. Yet, these bloggers earn very well. Blogger Jon Morrow has documented how he makes $100,000 a month from his blog. I asked him how. His answer was that no sell earns more than soft sell. 'Selling directly on your blog is a triple negative for your blog-based business: it ruins your engagement,' said Jon. 'When you provide useful content but then you turn it into a sales pitch at the end of the post, or you've got an ad, it stops people from commenting. They don't share your post in social media as much. It also doesn't convert [into sales] as well.'

"Jon and other blog ninjas only sell on emails, to their subscriber list. By keeping their blog pitch- and ad-free, they focus entirely on building rapport and engagement with their audience—getting those questions and comments, and responding to them. These blogs are positioned as free gold mines of advice. What reader doesn't love that? Then, when they approach subscribers to sell them something, more of them buy."

CAROL TICE, BUSINESS.TUTSPLUS.COM

EXPERT COMMENT

"Over the course of five years of blogging, I've earned over three million dollars without the use of aggressive selling tactics, product launches, or upsells.

"It's not that I'm not against hard selling and aggressive pitches.

"What I am against is not being truthful—both in terms of what is being offered, and how it's being offered (like false scarcity). There are nice ways to sell hard, and there are not-so-nice ways to sell hard. The moment dishonesty enters the selling equation is the moment you're selling for the wrong reasons.

"There's a time and a place for an honest hard sell, but in between there are several passive income opportunities for you which you can set up to run long-term on your site, and all it takes is 'teeing it up.'"

PAT FLYNN, WWW.SMARTPASSIVEINCOME.COM

#28 KNOW ALL THE RULES BEFORE YOU BEGIN

THE RULE

IT'S EASY TO MESS UP AND BREAK THE RULES, SO THE SMART BLOGGER LEARNS HOW TO DO IT BEFORE STARTING. THINK OF IT AS DUE DILIGENCE, OR A BUSINESS PLAN. JUST DON'T RUN BEFORE YOU CAN WALK. PREPARATION IS EVERYTHING!

Where it comes from:

You know that thing some people do when they buy a new phone, or TV, or computer? They look for the instruction manual. Not everyone does this, but for those who do, it can be a real shock to discover there isn't one. You might get a few setup instructions, but basically you're on your own, baby. It's a bit like that with blogging. There is help to be had online, of course—experts and advice galore—but it's hard to sift through it all, and hard to decide who or what to believe. The problem is, we all like to know the ground rules when faced with something new and unknown, and we want them to be as simple as possible. Shortcuts, instructions, tips, warnings—if they exist, we want to know them, but preferably in a list of no more than ten bullets (or 28, perhaps). When others have found out the hard way, why not learn from that?

WHEN TO BREAK THE RULE

Go ahead and break this rule any time. By now you've probably got the picture that there are no definitive rules for blogging. The rules in this book are one person's selection from any number of rules (or versions of rules) that exist, thanks to the collective reasoning, commenting, and opining of thousands, if not millions, of bloggers. For many of the rules, you can find those who both agree and disagree, often quite strongly—as you can see from the blogger stories and expert comments in this book.

There is nothing wrong with doing your own research and setting your own rules based on what makes sense to you and the nature of your blogging goals. But don't wait to get stuck in. The sooner you start blogging, learning from other bloggers, and figuring it out as you go along, the sooner you'll start having fun with blogging.

"The wonderful thing about the internet is there really ARE no rules. If it works for some, I guess that's great."

MARK W. SCHAEFER, WWW.BUSINESSESGROW.COM

RISK FACTOR: LOW

#28 KNOW ALL THE RULES BEFORE YOU BEGIN

BLOGGER STORY

"Learn the rules? But what rules? When I first had the thought to start a blog, I Googled 'how to blog for the super beginner.' Even that first search had me going cross-eyed with the rules, terminology, options, platforms, web hosts, layouts, and themes. I did hours and hours of research and finally ended up going with Blogger.com, which was extremely user friendly and a great place to start. I've completely changed the look of my blog five times since 2008 and now I self host, using WordPress (from WordPress.org—not at WordPress.com. There is a difference—why so many options!?).

"In the end, I've learned that it is far more fun to learn the rules as you go, there's always room for change and improvement. When it comes to blogging, I'd say that you should follow some rules but break most of them. Standing out is the idea!"

TARA MURRAY, WWW.MAMACHEE.COM

EXPERT COMMENT

"I kind of live my life by the idea of 'learn the rules in order to break the rules.' When you've been around a while, you'll notice that a lot of the same advice is given about how to run your blog. I know and understand why there are 'blogging rules' (or guidelines) in place.

"Most of the time, it's full of smart advice. Hell, I've given a lot of that advice on IFB! And yet, once you get the hang of blogging, understand your readers and what they respond to, you kind of learn…some of that advice isn't best for you and your site."

ASHLEY ROBISON, HEARTIFB.COM

ORDS

OUR RULES

THEY SAY THAT ENDINGS MATTER (#9), AND THE AIM OF THIS BOOK IS TO GET YOU THINKING—WHAT IS RIGHT FOR YOU AND YOUR BLOG? SO I'LL LEAVE YOU WITH SOME OF THE KEY POINTS:

"IF YOUR REASON FOR BLOGGING IS MORE TO DO WITH PLEASING YOURSELF RATHER THAN APPEALING TO OTHERS, GO AHEAD AND FORGET ABOUT THE TARGET AUDIENCE." (#1)

"ON A SELF-HOSTED BLOG, SECURITY IS DOWN TO YOU. THERE ARE MANY HAPPY IT PEOPLE MAKING A LIVING FROM SORTING OUT PEOPLE'S HACKED BLOGS." (#2)

"WATCHING THE NUMBERS CAN BE AN EMOTIONAL ROLLERCOASTER RIDE THAT FOR SOME PEOPLE TAKES AWAY THE JOY OF BLOGGING." (#4)

"A BLOG WRITTEN BY AN INDIVIDUAL IS USUALLY A FAR MORE PERSONAL FORM OF PUBLISHING THAN YOU FIND IN TRADITIONAL MEDIA—THIS CAN BE SOMETHING TO CELEBRATE." (#10)

"BLOGGING ABOUT CUPCAKES? THEN NO-ONE CARES WHAT YOU THINK OF THE LATEST BROADWAY SHOW." (#8)

"ENDING A BLOG POST ON A SALES PITCH IS FINE, BUT TRY TO VARY IT—AND THINK OF IT AS A NUDGE RATHER THAN A PUSH." (#9)

"SOME PEOPLE CAN MAKE SOME MONEY FROM BLOGGING, BUT ONLY A VERY SMALL PERCENTAGE MAKE A LOT OF MONEY FROM IT." (#24)

"IT'S CRUCIAL TO MEASURE THE RELEVANT THINGS AND NOT PAY UNDUE ATTENTION TO EVERYTHING ELSE." (#20)

"IF YOUR REASON FOR BLOGGING IS TO MAKE MONEY, YOU CAN'T AFFORD TO DASH OFF ANY OLD HEADLINE." (#14)

"DO YOU HAVE A VALID REASON TO STAY ANONYMOUS OR ARE YOU JUST A BIT SHY?" (#11)

"SOME PEOPLE BELIEVE YOU CAN NEVER OVERDO THE SELLING, BECAUSE SKY-HIGH SALES OUTWEIGH ANY NUMBER OF DISGRUNTLED PROSPECTS." (#27)

"JUST BECAUSE AN IMAGE OR A POEM OR A SONG HAS BEEN POSTED UMPTEEN TIMES ON VARIOUS SOCIAL NETWORKS, BLOGS, AND NEWS SITES, DON'T ASSUME IT'S FREE TO USE ON YOUR BLOG." (#18)

"CHOOSE YOUR BLOGGING BUDDIES WISELY." (#21)

"DON'T LEAVE DRIVE-BY COMMENTS LIKE 'GREAT POST!' UNLESS YOU WANT TO BE TAKEN FOR A SPAMMER." (#16)

RESOURCES:
BLOGGING TOOLS & FURTHER READING

GETTING GOING WITH BLOGGING/GENERAL ADVICE

WordPress—comparison of hosted vs. self-hosted versions:
http://en.support.wordpress.com/com-vs-org

BlogHer—blogging and social media tips:
http://www.blogher.com/blogher-topics/blogging-social-media

Copyblogger—online marketing advice, blogging wisdom,
e-books, and more:
http://www.copyblogger.com

ProBlogger—blog tips to help you make money blogging:
http://www.problogger.net

CONTENT

HubSpot's Blog Topic Generator:
http://www.hubspot.com/blog-topic-generator

Grammar Girl—Mignon Fogarty's friendly guide to the world
of grammar, punctuation, usage, and fun developments in the
English language:
http://www.quickanddirtytips.com/grammar-girl

How to Write Great Blog Content, from ProBlogger:
http://www.problogger.net/how-to-write-great-blog-content

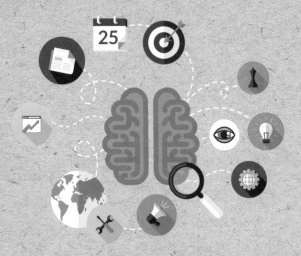

PRESENTATION

5 Design Tips to Boost Blog Conversions, by Brian Casel
at Mashable:
http://mashable.com/2013/07/19/blog-design-tips

20 Design Features That Will Make Your Blog Stand Out
From The Crowd, by Michael Dunlop at incomediary.com:
http://www.incomediary.com/make-your-blog-stand-out-
from-the-crowd

How Typography Affects Conversions, by Ankit Oberoi
at KissMetrics:
https://blog.kissmetrics.com/how-typography-affects-
conversions

Ow My Eyes—the case for not having white text on
a dark background:
http://www.ironicsans.com/owmyeyes

PROMOTING A BLOG

32 Experts Share Their Best Blog Post Promotion Tips,
by Kristi Hines at kikolani.com:
http://kikolani.com/blog-post-promotion-tips.html

Matt Cutts Clarifies Guest Blogging for SEO (with tips),
by John Rampton at SearchEngineJournal.com:
http://www.searchenginejournal.com/matt-cutts-clarifies-
guest-blogging-for-seo/86859

Can I Really Make a Living by Blogging, by Melanie Pinola
at LifeHacker.com:
http://lifehacker.com/can-i-really-make-a-living-by-
blogging-1537783554

ETIQUETTE

Top Tips for Blogger Etiquette, by Sally Whittle at tots100.co.uk:
http://www.tots100.co.uk/2013/09/17/top-tips-for-blogger-
etiquette

Blogger Etiquette—Dos and Don'ts:
http://blog.ifabbo.com/blogger-etiquette-dos-and-donts

KEEPING YOUR BLOG SECURE

9 Tips for WordPress Security, by Kim Crawley
at websynthesis.com:
http://websynthesis.com/advanced-wordpress-security

STAYING LEGAL

Legal Guide for Bloggers, from the Electronic Frontier
Foundation:
https://www.eff.org/issues/bloggers/legal

5 Rules about Using Web Images in your Blog, by Lance Godard
at SocialMediaToday.com:
http://www.socialmediatoday.com/content/5-rules-about-using-
web-images-your-blog

INDEX:

A

accessibility 59
advertising 10, 15, 17, 41, 62, 72, 103, 112, 114
analytics 15, 22
anonymity 48–51, 121
apps 16, 52, 108
attention spans 32, 60
avatars 48

B

backgrounds 56–59, 123
Blogger 12–13, 118
blogosphere 69, 83, 100
buddies 88–91, 121
bullet points 54
bulletin boards 48
business blogs 10, 16–17, 28, 33, 41, 46, 53, 62, 84, 86, 89, 102, 104, 114
business textbooks 8–10, 28, 36, 86

C

censorship 49
clean style 72–75
click-through rates 60–61
clip art 53
clutter 72–75
collaboration 89
color palettes 59, 73
comments 9, 21–22, 40, 46, 68–71, 96–97, 114, 121
community-building 10, 14, 47, 67, 69–70, 87–91
competition 21, 82, 88, 95

composition 55
contact details 48, 50
contrast 56
copyright 77, 79, 89
cost 13–14
creative blogs 16, 53
credits 76–77

D

dark web 48, 57, 59
deadlines 20
design 13, 16, 39, 53, 55, 58–59, 72–75, 85, 109, 123
Digg 109

E

eCommerce 15, 102
email 43, 87, 104–7, 114
engagement 96–99
experiments 9, 55
eyestrain 57, 59, 123

F

Facebook 21–22, 44, 66, 68–69, 76, 108–10
fair usage 76
Flickr 52
follow-up boxes 69
free 13–15, 18, 55, 77, 82, 88, 92, 105, 113–114
functionality 15

G

goals 10, 20–21, 23, 52–53, 85, 87, 97, 99, 113, 117
Google+ 68, 109–10
Google Analytics 22
grammar 28–31, 53, 122

group blogging 91
guest posts 37, 68, 70, 89, 92–96

H

hacked blogs 13, 120
hard selling 112–15
headings 54, 59–63, 78, 81, 121
hobby bloggers 7, 17, 44, 85–86
hosted blogs 12–13, 122
HubSpot 109, 122

I

images 52–55, 121, 125
Instagram 52, 108
intellectual property 76–79
IT people 13, 120

K

keywords 34, 78, 80–83, 94

L

libel 89
lighting 55
LinkedIn 68, 110
long posts 32–35

M

MailChimp 105
marketing 8, 40, 46, 86, 95–96, 102, 105–7, 112–15, 122
metadata 81
metrics 15, 63, 86, 123
mind-set 16–19
minimalism 72–75
money-making 100–103, 121

N

newsletters 104–8
niches 36–39, 81,
    89, 93

O

off-topic posts 37, 39,
    44, 46
other blogs 68–71,
    77–78, 81, 88–95, 117

P

paragraphs 54, 57, 81
photo-editing tools 55
Pinterest 52
plagiarism 79
plug-ins 14, 43, 81
power words 60–61
preparation 116–19
privacy 44
pro bloggers 7, 12,
    15–19, 24–25, 27–28,
    60, 68, 100–103

Q

questions 40–43, 66

R

reblogging 77–78
record-keeping 9, 11
regular posts 24–27
routines 26

S

scrapers 79
search-engine
    optimization (SEO)
    34, 40, 80–83,
    92–95, 124
searches 12, 23–25,
    32, 34, 50, 68,
    80–83, 92–95

second blogs 37
security 13, 120,
    124–25
self-hosting 12–15,
    118, 120, 122
serif fonts 59
sharing 108–11
short posts 32–35,
    46, 57, 110
sidebars 16
SMART goals 20–21
social media 20, 44–46,
    48, 52, 54, 64–69,
    76, 81, 94, 96, 108,
    110–11, 113–14,
    121–22
software 12–13, 20, 79
spam 13, 48, 68–69, 87,
    95, 104–105, 112–113
spelling 28–31
spiders 68
sponsored posts 19
statistics 20–23, 47, 81,
    84–85, 109
stealing 76–79
stock images 53–54
style switchers 59
summaries 43

T

tags 81
target audiences 8–11,
    36, 56–57, 59, 61,
    85, 93, 96–99, 112,
    119–20
templates 12–13,
    16, 73
text 56–59, 123
themes 13–14, 57,
    73, 118
topics 36–39, 44–47,
    69, 81, 122

Tumblr 13, 52
Twitter 22, 66, 68,
    108, 110, 113
typefaces 57, 60, 123

U

updates 14, 34, 66,
    81, 105, 110
upgrades 13

V

visitor numbers 9,
    20–22, 24–25,
    60–61, 81–82,
    84–87, 92, 96, 120

W

widgets 16, 72–73, 108
WordPress 12–14, 43,
    118, 122, 124
Wordtracker 83
writing skills 9, 11,
    26–27, 30–31,
    83, 91

Y

Yoast 81
YouTube 102

ACKNOWLEDGMENTS:

I would like to thank everyone at Ilex Press, in particular Roly Allen for the initial idea and Rachel Silverlight for her cheerful patience throughout the project. My thanks also to my agent, Charlotte Howard of Fox & Howard Literary Agency, to my husband Nick, and of course to all the fantastic experts, mavericks, and blogging rule-breakers who contributed their insights and opinions.

PICTURE CREDITS:

Illustrations by Venimo, Tarchyshnik Andrei, PureSolution, Dooder, Arcady, Jcsmilly, Vasabii, Tovovan, totallyPic.com, and Jane Kelly—all courtesy of Shutterstock.